Paranormal
CUMBRIA

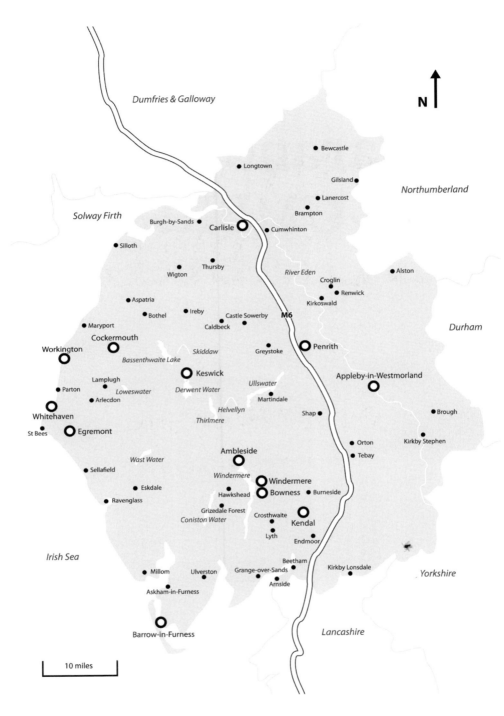

Cumbria, showing the areas mentioned in the text. (Map by Jenni Wilson)

Paranormal
CUMBRIA

To Josh

GEOFF HOLDER

Enjoy Exploring

The
History
Press

*To Jim Templeton, who took the photograph of the 'Solway Spaceman' in 1964,
and has generously shared the mystery with the world ever since.*

First published 2012

The History Press
The Mill, Brimscombe Port
Stroud, Gloucestershire, GL5 2QG
www.thehistorypress.co.uk

British Library Cataloguing in Publication Data.
A catalogue record for this book is available from the British Library.

ISBN 978 0 7524 5412 2

Typesetting and origination by The History Press
Printed in Great Britain
Manufacturing managed by Jellyfish Print Solutions Ltd

CONTENTS

ACKNOWLEDGEMENTS

The author wishes to thank the following for their contributions and assistance: Linden Adams; Andy Altmann at www.whynotassociates.com; Alan Cleaver (www.strangebritain.co.uk); Cumbria County Council Library Services (Local Studies); the 5-Plus-1 pub quiz team at the George and Dragon, Garrigill; Gordon Hudson; Owen Lightburn; Dominic Strange; Jim Templeton; Tullie House Museum; The *Whitehaven News*; Gordon Young (www.gordonyoung.net); and the team at The History Press, especially Cate Ludlow. Jennie Wilson did the map while the long-suffering, yet remarkably radiant Ségolène Dupuy worked on the images.

This book is part of a series of similar works on mysteries, the paranormal and the strange. To find out more, or to discover how to contribute your own experience, go to www.geoffholder.com.

INTRODUCTION

Viewed through the right filter, Cumbria can be seen as a cauldron of mysteries both ancient and modern. To take just two examples, in the seventeenth century Warwickshire minister Samuel Clarke, author of *A Mirror or Looking Glass Both for Saints and Sinners*, described how during the Civil War the sky rained blood in Cumberland, covering a church and churchyard with red ichor as an omen of disaster. And on 12 January 2007 and 22 February 2010 the *News & Star* and the *Cumberland News* respectively reported that car key fobs were mysteriously refusing to work on Esk Street and Swan Street in Longtown, and Crescent Road in Windermere. Not anywhere else, just those streets. 'It is as if you have come to some sort of black hole for cars,' said one witness.

Paranormal Cumbria is a companion volume to *The Guide to the Mysterious Lake District,* which I wrote in 2009. In that book I took a village-by-village, lake-by-lake, geographical approach to everything strange, supernatural, magical and marvellous. Here, with all new material, I cover the whole of Cumbria, not just the National Park area, and the chapters are arranged thematically. So new (or at least re-excavated) information is presented on the Croglin Vampire and its lesser-known cousin the Renwick Cockatrice. We look at witchcraft and folk magic from the seventeenth century to the present day, followed by a 'cultural history' of the saga of the 'Cursing Stone' of Carlisle. Chapter Four rescues a number of amazing episodes of psychic powers from obscure books and specialist journals, while the following chapter presents an astonishing series of twentieth-century sightings of fairies and other beings. In Chapter Six, Cumbria also seems home to an entire menagerie of mysterious creatures, from big cats and black dogs to escaped wolves and lake monsters. And we finish by delving deep into the enduring mystery of the Solway Spaceman.

In setting out these explorations, I have been conscious of two overriding elements: firstly, stories about the paranormal are easily among the most unreliable in the non-fiction canon, being prone to everything from sins of omission and exaggeration to outright invention and even hoaxing. For this reason I have not only given all my sources, but also, wherever possible, I have dug through all the accumulated layers of retelling and reworking in secondary works, back to the earliest original printed accounts for each individual case. That way you can check if I have been accurate and honest, and also see whether you agree with my interpretation. There is also a compete bibliography at the back of the book.

Secondly, there is the role of the media in transmitting these accounts. Most of us do not have direct experiences of the strange and supernatural, so the way we learn about all these stories depends on some kind of medium, whether this is a hefty Victorian volume or a blogger's website. When a story appears in print or on the screen for the first time, it has an impact on the way people interpret the event thereafter; the media can therefore not merely *deliver* these stories, but also *shape* them, particularly if there is a commercial or political agenda at play. Don't take everything at face value.

A quick note for those unfamiliar with the geography. The county of Cumbria, created in 1974, incorporates the former counties of Cumberland and Westmorland – which is why those names crop up so much – as well as a good slice of territory taken from Lancashire, and small parcels of land that used to belong to Yorkshire and Northumberland.

Cumbria is a wonderful part of the world, and I contend that the mysteries and weirdness presented here enhance that sense of wonder. Enjoy exploring.

Geoff Holder, 2012

CHAPTER ONE

THE CROGLIN VAMPIRE AND THE RENWICK COCKATRICE

THE VAMPIRE OF CROGLIN GRANGE

This story is one of the most enduring – and misrepresented – of all of Cumbria's legends. At its core is a darkly Gothic tale of a sister and two brothers who lease a house in the remote fellside country of northeast Cumbria. On two separate occasions, nine months apart, a vampire-like being enters the girl's bedroom and attacks her, breaking her skin with its teeth. During the second attack one of the brother wounds the 'vampire' in the leg. A search of a vault in the local

The fellside road into Croglin. (© Geoff Holder)

churchyard reveals a corpse-like figure with a bullet lodged in one leg. The creature is burned to ashes and the attacks stop. The story has been repeated and embellished over the years, and by a process of Chinese whispers has become distorted and exaggerated. By going back over the various accounts I think I may have solved part of the mystery. But to get to that point, we need to revisit the tortuous history of the Croglin Vampire.

THE ORIGINAL STORY – 1874–1900

The vampire first appeared in print in Volume 4 of *The Story of My Life*, a diary and journal published by Augustus Hare in 1900. Hare (1834–1903) was a well-heeled socialite and author of numerous travel books on some of the more agreeable areas of Europe. His autobiography is full to the brim of anecdotes of where he met this princess or that baron, and which peer of the realm he happened to have dinner with last night. He was also an inveterate gossip, and loved to write down entertaining snippets told to him by his fashionable acquaintances. As an established raconteur in high society, Hare was skilled at reshaping the stories he had been told, often making them more dramatic than in the original. This same gift for oratory and storytelling meant that he was often notoriously light on reliable details. He had a particular fondness for ghost stories, especially those that had a sting in the tale, or conveyed the appropriate sense of spine-chilling *frisson*. The tale of the Vampire of Croglin was one such episode.

On 24 June 1874, Hare dined with Captain Edward Fisher-Rowe, who was Hare's neighbour in Surrey and was getting married to Hare's cousin, Lady Victoria Liddel in five days' time; they later went on to have six children, one of whom lived until 1958. Also present was Fisher-Rowe's soon-to-be father-in-law, Henry Thomas Liddell, the 1st Earl of Ravensworth. Lord Ravensworth told a creepy story of a death omen he had heard from the Lowlands of Scotland, and Hare no doubt contributed one of his polished anecdotes. Captain Fisher (as Hare styled him) felt compelled to participate and so contributed two episodes – a standard ghost story of a phantom carriage and death banshee, which no one now remembers, and the vampire tale, which has achieved worldwide fame. In Fisher's tale, as recorded and possibly reworked by Hare, Fisher's family owned an old house in Cumberland named Croglin Grange, but when they moved south they let it to three siblings. The story then proceeded as given above.

This, then, is the origin story for the Croglin Vampire, the basis for everything that follows. At this point, a few matters should be mentioned: the story is not a first-hand account by a witness, but an after-dinner ghost story told by Captain Fisher and then written down by Hare some time later. It is therefore third-hand at the very least, with all that implies for the possibility of changes and exaggeration. Furthermore, Fisher (according to Hare) gave no dates, and did not mention the name of the family concerned. In this it conforms to a standard kind of ghost story, one told for entertainment where the narrative is more important than mere details. I also point out that between 1874 and 1900, many works on Cumbrian folklore and local history had been published, and none of them mention the story. Of course, absence of evidence is not evidence of absence, but it is perhaps significant that the *only* original source of the Croglin Vampire in print is in Hare's journal of gossip.

THE LEAP INTO PUBLIC CONSCIOUSNESS:
CHARLES HARPER, 1907

The vampire story first reached a wider audience when it was printed *verbatim* in Charles Harper's sceptically-minded book *Haunted Houses*, published in 1907. In the Fisher and Hare account, Croglin Grange overlooked the churchyard. Harper visited Croglin and discovered that (a) there is no place named Croglin Grange, only Croglin High Hall and Low Hall (he thought the latter was the building indicated in Fisher's narrative); (b) Croglin Low Hall was well over a mile from the church; and (c) the churchyard contained no tomb or mausoleum that resembled the vault where the vampire was supposed to have taken refuge, and where it met its doom. In other words, he found that the geography of the tale as set out by Fisher bore little resemblance to the actual situation at Croglin.

THE PENNY DREADFUL CONNECTION? – 1929

In 1929, Montague Summers, a prolific and popular if somewhat credulous chronicler of the supernatural, again printed the original story word-for-word in his book *The Vampire in Europe*. He countered some of Harper's criticisms, suggesting that the vault had been deliberately destroyed to erase all trace of the vampire episode. Summers also reprinted a chapter from *Varney the Vampire*, a low-brow and sensational 'penny dreadful' novel written by James Malcolm Rymer in 1847. Summers did not comment on the several similarities – in action, characterisation and description – between the Croglin Vampire and the manner in which Varney enters a room and attacks a female victim.

THE PERIOD OF INVENTION – 1950s

During the middle decades of the twentieth century the vampire story was repeated in a number of popular publications, and in so doing gained a number of entirely invented elements (a typical example was *Unsolved Mysteries*, written by Valentine Dyall, 'The Man in Black', in 1954). The two brothers and sister were said to be Australian, and the female victim's first name was given as Amelia. And the events were meant to have taken place in 1875, or at least the late

Croglin Low Hall. (From Charles Harper's
Haunted Houses, 1907)

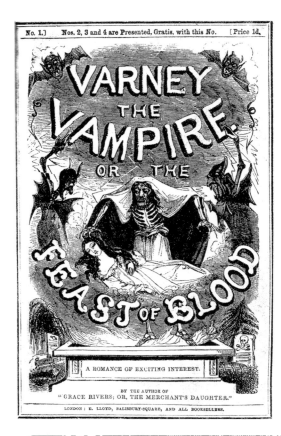

The front cover of the first issue of the 'penny dreadful'. (*Varney the Vampire*, 1847)

The vampire attacks its female victim. (From the first issue of *Varney the Vampire*, 1845)

nineteenth century. None of these details are mentioned in the original account, and – despite the fact that they are now all established aspects of the legend, endlessly repeated in websites and pop-horror books – they are all entirely false.

HARE AND FISHER JUSTIFIED? – F. CLIVE-ROSS' INVESTIGATION, 1962

In November 1962 F. Clive-Ross, a writer interested in matters mystical and mysterious, journeyed to Croglin to undertake what was probably the first on-the-spot research for many decades. Through contact with several local people, including Mrs Mary Watson, the tenant of Croglin Low Hall, and Mrs Parkin, the widow of Inglewood Parkin, the former owner of the estate on which Low Hall stood, Clive-Ross uncovered a number of illuminating elements:

1. The tradition was well-known locally, so much so that the former Chief Constable of Cumberland and Westmorland enjoyed 'reconstructing the crime' when he was a member of shooting parties taking lunch at Croglin Low Hall. Mrs Watson showed Clive-Ross the very window that the vampire was said to have climbed through.

2. The tenants who had suffered the vampire attacks were described as coming from outside the local area, and having the surname Cranswell.

3. A local member of the Fisher family who had been born in the 1860s remembered hearing the tale from his grandparents, so if the events were in any way real they dated from at least the early 1800s, if not much earlier. Another Fisher family member in Surrey recalled that her aunt would retell the story every Christmas. Clearly the vampire was a long-standing Fisher family tradition.

4. According to the deeds of Croglin Low Hall, the farm was sometimes referred to as Croglin Grange before 1720. Up to the same date the now two-storey building had just one storey, which matched the description given by Captain Fisher.

5. The main village of Croglin, where the present church stands, was once known as Croglin Multa. The church of Croglin Parva had once stood next to Croglin Low Hall, but it was destroyed during the Civil War in the seventeenth century. In 1933, this church field was still littered with good-quality stones that were later re-used in local buildings. (Later research shows that Croglin Parva church appears on both John Speed's 1610 map of Cumberland and Blaeu's map of 1667.) Tradition spoke of graves in the field, including the Fisher vault. If all this was true, then this long-vanished churchyard was the one featured in the Fisher/Hare narrative. The current church over a mile away in Croglin village has nothing to do with the vampire story.

Based on the above, and the opinions of Mrs Parkin and others, Clive-Ross concluded that the vampire legend had not been invented as a dinner-party anecdote, but whatever had kickstarted it – an event whose details were sadly lost to history – it must have taken place sometime around the 1680s to the 1690s, some two centuries before what had by now falsely become the 'established' date for the vampire attack. His article also revealed that in the 1950s an ancient human skeleton was accidentally discovered at Low Hall, hidden behind the dining room fireplace. Its provenance was a mystery, although it seemed that it had previously been noticed (and left undisturbed) in 1928. Even more intriguing from the point of view of research into the vampire, he found a tradition linking Croglin High Hall to the story. The tenant there had found what he thought were rat bites on the throat of his three-year-old daughter. She became frightened, sickly and pale, and only when the attacks took place on their neighbour were the bitemarks reassessed. The tenant, who was not named, was one of those who took part in the destruction of the loathsome visitant. F. Clive-Ross published his findings in the relatively obscure magazine *Tomorrow* in Spring 1963, and his article became the benchmark for years to come. When Lionel Fanthorpe investigated the case in the 1970s (published in *The World's Greatest Unsolved Mysteries*) he largely substantiated Clive-Ross' findings although he did not pick up on the expansion of the story into High Hall.

THE PLOT THICKENS – MARC ALEXANDER, 1970

In 1970 journalist and author Marc Alexander made the journey to Croglin. He appeared to be unaware of Clive-Ross' article, but he too spoke to Mrs Watson and in the course of showing him around Croglin Low Hall she told him basically the same information she had given his predecessor eight years' previously. When he came to write up the visit in *Haunted Churches & Abbeys of Britain* (1978), however, Alexander had a veritable bombshell: he had an entirely different vampire tradition, a new date and location for the events – and even an identity for the vampire.

Croglin parish church, with the fells in the background and sheep in the graveyard. The present-day church has no connections with the vampire legend. (© Geoff Holder)

The revelation came in a letter he included from the Revd Dr Matthew Roberts, the rector of Croglin from 1944 to 1948. Revd Roberts had heard the following tale from the Revd Reginald Green, rector from 1891 to 1907. According to the story, one of the beautiful daughters of the Revd Joseph Ireland, rector from 1804 to 1837, was asleep in her home in Croglin village when she was attacked by something that drew blood from her neck. The following night the same thing happened. On the third night the girl's brothers set a trap, with one lurking outside the door of his sister's room, and the other hiding in the stable yard. When the girl screamed the lad rushed in – to find a large black bat flapping around the bed. He drove it out of the window, where the other brother shot it. Wounded, the bat flew low into the churchyard and under the flat table-tomb of George Sanderson – the rector from 1671 to 1691. The story finished in the traditional manner, with the body of the minister being exhumed and a stake driven through its heart.

Although some of the elements in this variant conform to what we might term the 'mainstream' version of the legend, others are clearly anomalous. The location is shifted from Croglin Low Hall to Croglin village; the victim is different; the date is moved to the early 1800s; the transformation to a flying bat is mentioned for the first time (could there be some thematic or folkloric connection with the Renwick 'bat' described below?); and the vampire is identified as a former minister who lived in the 1680s, the very period when the originating events might have occurred.

I am, however, a tad sceptical. The entire scenario sounds as if it has been taken wholesale from either Bram Stoker's novel *Dracula* or one of the film adaptations such as *Nosferatu* (1922) or the 1931 Hollywood *Dracula* starring Bela Lugosi. The only original element is the identification of George Sanderson as the undead assailant. One of the intriguing aspects of the whole episode is that Mr Alexander's research has been virtually ignored, and most popular summaries of the Croglin case make no mention of his valuable work; I am pleased to do my small part in restoring his discoveries to public gaze.

ENTER THE TOWRYS –
RICHARD WHITTINGTON-EGAN'S RESEARCH, 2005

In June 2005 the widely-published author Richard Whittington-Egan reviewed the case for the *Contemporary Review*. Going back through the records he established that Croglin Low Hall was sold by the Howard family to George Towry in 1688. The Towrys owned the property until 1727, when it was sold to a Mr Johnson. It was only in 1809 that the Fisher family took possession of Low Hall, and then not as owners – as Captain Fisher-Rowe had told Hare – but as tenants. So if the unknown events that instigated the vampire legend took place as surmised in the 1680s/90s, then it was the Towrys who were living at Low Hall at the time. This means that not only could there have been no 'Fisher vault' in the now-vanished Croglin Parma church, but also that the victims of the 'vampire' (or whatever it was) were not the Fishers but the Towrys. Whittington-Egan speculated that the Fishers had been told the story by the departing or soon-to-be deceased Towrys, and had then incorporated it into their own family mythology.

PRESENT DAY – A VAMPIRE FOR ALL SEASONS

The Croglin Vampire is now a permanent fixture in popular culture. There is the inevitable panoply of websites and newspaper articles. In 2008 best-selling children's author Terry Deary wrote a book on it. And in December 2007 the Lakeland Players put on a village pantomime

A scene from the 2007 pantomime 'The Pirates of Watermillock and the Legend of the Croglin Vampire'. From left to right: Ellen Jones, Frank Little as undead French hairdresser Vam 'Pierre, and Elaine Tyson. (Courtesy of Owen Lightburn)

entitled 'The Pirates of Watermillock and the Legend of the Croglin Vampire'. Written and directed by local drama student Owen Lightburn, it took the usual panto liberties with the story, so that two rival sets of pirates were seeking the monster, who turned out to be a world-class French hairdresser called Croglin Vam'Pierre. Well, it made me laugh.

CONCLUSION

Can anything firm be concluded about the entire vampire farrago? Augustus Hare, the original printed source, may not be entirely reliable in his details – and yet the legend clearly appears to be of longstanding in the Croglin area, dating back according to the Fishers themselves at least 200 years. If some kind of originating event did take place in the late seventeenth century, it may have been experienced by the Towrys, not their successors the Fishers, whose family folklore it then became. We have two (or even three) locations for the attacks, and three different female victims from two different eras. We have a human (or human-like) figure, and in one variant a transformation into a bat. We have elements that seem to be shared with popular works such as *Varney the Vampire* and *Dracula*. There is no original documentation and, to be frank, everything that anyone has written on the subject – including this very chapter – is based on little more than various degrees of hearsay and oral tradition. I suspect that if Augustus Hare had not jotted down his neighbour's after-dinner story in 1874 then very few people outside the fellside villages would have ever heard of the Croglin Vampire.

However, there is one possibility that I would like to float as a potential starter for future research. Much of the collected traditions point to the origin events taking place in the 1680s or 1690s, while Marc Alexander's researches identified the Revd George Sanderson as the actual vampire. I wonder whether we are actually looking at a distorted view of a seventeenth-century religious dispute. During the Commonwealth, after Charles I had been executed and England was effectively a republic from 1649 to 1660, the Puritan regime imposed many ministers on parishes across the country. Such men were known as 'intruding vicars' and George Sanderson was one such, having been 'intruded' into the parish of Gainford in Durham in 1652. When the Commonwealth fell and Charles II was restored to the throne, the 1662 Act of Conformity required all vicars to toe the new party line, leading some 2,000 Puritan ministers to quit their parishes, an event known as the Great Ejection. As noted in *The Ejected of 1662 in Cumberland & Westmorland*, a compendium published by the University of Manchester, George Sanderson was happy to change his spots, and agitated to replace one of the ejected vicars in Cumberland. In 1671, now a monarchy-supporting Church of England vicar, he got the job at Croglin and Kirkoswald, remaining as rector of Croglin until his death in 1691.

Is it possible that some people in the Croglin area were displeased that the Revd Sanderson had abjured his Puritan principles and replaced their former minister? Could this have led to some kind of rumour mill against the rector, a campaign that somehow became twisted into the vampire tale? As with everything else concerning the Croglin Vampire, this is pure speculation. The entire tale is an enduring mystery – and a mystery, so far, with no solution.

THE RENWICK COCKATRICE

The village of Renwick, southeast of Croglin, has a peculiar legend which states that when the local church was being renovated, a flying monster recognised as a cockatrice flew out. All the terrified villagers fled with the exception of one doughty fellow, John Tallentire, who struck the creature down with a branch of rowan (rowan is the traditional apotropaic wood used to keep away witches, fairies and evil spirits). As a result, the Tallentires were supposedly exempted from paying tithes in later years. Over time the story has evolved to the point where the lethal cockatrice has been bowdlerised into just a large bat, with the consequence that the villagers have long been known as 'Renwick Bats'.

The cockatrice is often confused with another mythical monster, the basilisk, a giant snake-like creature whose most recent appearance has been in the *Harry Potter* books and films. The cockatrice proper was believed to be produced when a cockerel in the last years of its life laid an egg; this egg had some mystical attraction for toads and snakes, and if one of these creatures were to sit on the cock's egg and incubate it, a hybrid being would hatch out, with the head and comb of a cockerel and the rear-parts of a dragon, snake or amphibian. The breath and blood of a cockatrice was fatally poisonous, and in some versions, like the basilisk, its gaze could kill or turn the victims to stone. Cockatrices were not mere quaint folklore, however: up until the seventeenth century they were firmly believed in. In 1474 a tribunal in the Swiss town of Basle put a cockerel on trial; it was found guilty of laying an egg, and both bird and egg were burnt in the market place, with the assembled throng of townspeople giving thanks that the hazard had been averted before a toad could brood upon the egg. Writers of natural history from Roman times to the Renaissance give detailed descriptions of the cockatrice's habits, and the word appears several times in the Old Testament, for example:

Renwick parish church, built long after the long-rumoured cockatrice incident. (© Geoff Holder)

> Out of the serpent's nest shall come forth a cockatrice, and his fruit shall be a fiery flying serpent. (Isaiah 14:29)
>
> For, behold, I will send serpents, cockatrices among you, which will not be charmed, and they shall bite you, saith the Lord. (Jeremiah 8:17)

As for the Renwick cockatrice, the tale has grown in the telling. Its first appearance is in William Hutchinson's *History of the County of Cumberland*, published in 1794:

> All the proprietors [in Renwick] pay a prescription in lieu of tithes, except the owner of one estate [John Tallentire, of Scale Houses], who has a total exemption, derived from a circumstance which happened about 200 years ago, almost too ridiculous to be rehearsed or credited. The ancient possessor is said to have slain a noxious cockatrice, which the vulgar call a *crack-a-christ* at this day, as they rehearse the simple fable. There is some record [said to be dated 7th of James I], which the owner of the estate holds to testify his exemption, perhaps in a language or letter not to be understood by the villagers; and which he is too tenacious to suffer to be read by curious visitors.

Hutchinson got this information from the Notes supplied to him by John Housman, the son of a gardener at Corby Castle who was born in 1764. Housman published his own work – *A Topographical Description of Cumberland, Westmorland and Lancashire* – six years after Hutchinson's pioneering volume, but he does not tell us where he learned about the cockatrice. Peter Burn also mentions the incident in *English Border Ballads* (1876) but adds no additional detail, although by this date the cockatrice had transmogrified into the bat.

A cockatrice. (From *Fictitious & Symbolic Creatures in Art*, by John Vinycomb, 1909)

Hutchinson and Housman's original description contains some important clues. The event is said to have happened perhaps around the 1590s, a period when belief in cockatrices had not yet been exterminated in country districts. *Crack-a-christ* refers not to Jesus Christ but to the 'crist' or cockerel's comb said to spring from the head of the cockatrice. And we learn that in the 1790s the owner of the Tallentire estate had some mysterious document that he claimed exempted him from tithes (a tithe being one-tenth of the annual produce of the land, paid by parishioners to the parish church). Crucially, the canny farmer refused to show this document to anyone. This document is said to be dated '7th of James I', that is, the seventh year of the reign of King James I, which would be 1610 – more-or-less contemporary with the supposed ballpark date for the event.

The 'History of Renwick', a loose-leaf document written by local historian Richard Brocklington and kept in Renwick church, notes that a John Tallentyre appears in a document about building materials in 1608. In 1635, George Tallentire was the freeholder of Scalehouses, a local farm, and the Tallentires held the title until about 1875. The surname is still extant in the area. Brocklington also discovered that the 1842 Tithe Schedule had nothing to say about the Tallentires being exempted from paying tithes. The alleged document of John Tallentire from the 1790s has never been found. I have a suggestion, however. The National Archives hold a series of papers relating to the Hearth Tax, a tax on chimneys and fireplaces instigated by Charles II in 1662 (it was abolished in 1689). The tax was unpopular and widely flouted, one of the standard practices of avoidance being to present certificates of exemption on grounds of poverty or the low rentable value of specific properties. Roll E179/326/6 in the National Archives gives a long list of those exempted in Cumberland in 1673; and the Tallentire property is mentioned. Perhaps this exemption was what the estate owner in the 1790s was referring to, while cannily making sure no one actually inspected his spurious tax-free certificate.

In an unrelated section, Hutchinson noted that the church at Renwick had been renovated in 1733. Later writers conflated the two elements, so that in, for example, *Bulmer's History & Directory of Cumberland,* published in 1901, the cockatrice is said to have flown out of the ruins during the 1733 demolition; Hutchinson, however, makes no mention of this – like the story of the Croglin Vampire bat, it is a later invention.

Although we can trace the cockatrice back to its first appearance in print, and strip away some of the later accretions to the story, we still have no idea what the villagers of Renwick encountered back in the late sixteenth century. Perhaps some fearsome creature was indeed fought off by a brave farmer, and the story then grew in the telling. Or perhaps the whole thing was just made up as part of a landowner's tax-avoidance scheme.

A vampire bat. (From *The Imperial Dictionary*, 1855)

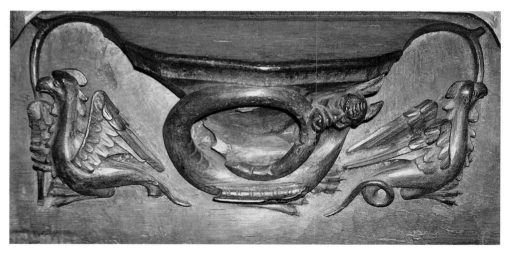

A pair of cockatrices flank a serpentine dragon on a misericord in the south choir stalls of Carlisle Cathedral. (Courtesy of Dominic Strange)

CHAPTER TWO

WITCHCRAFT, MAGIC AND THE DEVIL

WITCHCRAFT IN THE SEVENTEENTH CENTURY

Witchcraft was made a capital crime in England in 1541. In 1637, Charles I granted Carlisle its governing Charter, which, among other things, appointed two aldermen of the city to act as justices of the peace with wide-ranging powers to investigate:

> All manner of felonies, poisonings, enchantments, witchcrafts, magic art, trespasses, forstallings, regratings, engrossings and extortions whatsoever.

And in the Audit Books of the city for 1649-50 can be found the following entry:

> Itm for ye witchfynder £6 10s.

However, unlike some other counties, such as Essex, the Home Counties and Lancashire – not to mention much of Scotland – Cumbria largely escaped the worst excesses of the witch persecution, and indeed there are relatively few reliable records of investigations into 'enchantments, witchcrafts, magic art' in the area. And as for the 'witchfynder', this is a puzzling entry, because £6 10s was a large sum at the time, and yet there is no record of anyone actually performing the task. These references, by the way, come from *The Royal Charters of the City of Carlisle*, written by the former mayor, R.S. Ferguson, in 1894.

Documentary evidence for belief in witchcraft in the seventeenth century largely comes from legal trials. In many cases these trial records are annoyingly incomplete. We know, for example, that on 12 April 1659 Anne Thompson, a widow from Winton, was called before the General Sessions of the Public Peace at Appleby, accused of bewitching Margaret Bousefield, a spinster from the same area. The event had allegedly taken place on 14 February, and nineteen witnesses were called to prove the case. The details of the actual bewitchment are vague, and it appears that Mrs Thompson was released without the case continuing further. In 1675, John Robinson of Rowray in the parish of Lamplugh was said to have invoked 'evil spirits' in an attempt to locate hidden treasure (such divination for money was a common, if relatively minor, crime of the period). And in 1685, Thomasin Thomson, a widow of Ruckcroft in the parish of Ainstable in East Cumbria, was said to have bewitched to death a steer and two cows (each valued at 10s) belonging to Lancelot Young. (As with all the cases collected here, the details come from Cecil L'Estrange Ewen's book *Witchcraft and Demonism*.)

Much more detail appears in the case brought against Elizabeth Howe on 28 August 1672. Elizabeth was the wife of John Howe of Thursby. With Thomas Denton JP on the bench, several of the Howes' neighbours proceeded to accuse Elizabeth of sundry enchantments. John Robinson of Mooreend started off by stating that he had known the accused for twelve years and considered her to be, 'a person of evil life and conversation and suspected of doing many injuries to her neighbours and that by some witchcraft or evil art used by her.' Two years previously Elizabeth had fallen out with him over the price of some ploughing he had done for her; and a fortnight later his horse died in the plough. A year on, when Elizabeth saw his new cow and calf, she prophesied that, 'he would not get much good out of her.' True to the prediction, the cow became ill and had to be killed, and the calf died – all, John Robinson believed, because of Elizabeth Howe's witchcraft. The horse was worth 40s, the cow half that, and the calf 5s.

Other witnesses had similar stories. Around 1668, the cow of John Coultherd of Thursby died shortly after Elizabeth milked her without his permission. The cow was worth 50s. Joseph Williamson of Mooreend testified that Elizabeth had put her hand into his corn at Carlisle market, and that when he got home he suffered from fits so badly that it took three men to hold him down. His sickness lasted two months and he said that he did 'always think and conceive in his mind that she had gotten some power of him.' Edward Howe of Thursby – possibly a relation – stated that his wife Anne fell sick just after Elizabeth had visited them, and that during her week-long illness Anne often saw the witch's head peeping in on her. And Grace, wife of John Clemetson of Thursby, told the court that her son John was bewitched by Elizabeth, and that during his two-week-long illness he cried out that the witch was pulling his heart out. Both Anne Howe and John Clemetson got better when they 'blooded' Elizabeth. That is, the witch was brought to their respective homes and they cut her with a knife on the forehead. This was a traditional and widespread way of breaking a spell or curse. Grace Clemetson's son 'rose up out of bed and got blood of her, and presently after found great ease of his torments' while Edward Howe believed that if his wife had not blooded the witch, she would have died of her illness within 24 hours.

In its way, Elizabeth Howe's is typical of low-level witchcraft cases from right across the country; there was a dispute between neighbours, a virulent combination of clashing personalities and rows over money; the woman at the centre of the disputes had a long-established reputation for witchery; and so when animals and people fell ill – as they sometimes do, in distressing but quite natural ways – the link was made between the witch and sickness. Eventually the local ill-feeling reached boiling point and someone advanced the name of John Howe's wife to the authorities, who were obliged to investigate.

Elizabeth Howe was acquitted of all charges. In this she was lucky, as by 1672 a general scepticism about the reality of witchcraft was starting to creep into trial proceedings, and convictions were becoming fewer. In an earlier time and another place her fate may have been rather more unpleasant.

'STRANGE AND TRUE NEWS FROM WESTMORELAND'

The Devil makes an unusual appearance in a ballad first published in London in 1663. Entitled 'Strange and True News from Westmoreland', the truly strange supernatural contents are admirably summed up in its own lengthy subtitle:

> Being a true relation of one Gabriel Harding, who coming home drunk, struck his wife a blow on the breast and killed her out right; then did he forswear the evil deed which he knew himself guilty of. Likewise how a stranger did come to the house clothed in green, the people that were eye witness said it was an angel. Likewise how the stranger or angel did give sentence upon the man for killing of his wife. Also how Satan did break the man's neck that did forswear himself; and the stranger or angel did command Satan to hurt none else, and to vanish: which being done, there was a pleasant harmony of music heard to sound: then did the stranger clothed in green, take his leave of the people; whereof the chiefest in the parish desired it might be put in print, and have hereunto set their hands. To the tune of, In Summer Time.

An image used in *The Devil in Britain and America* (John Ashton, 1896) to show Gabriel Harding killing his wife, with the Devil looking on.

Yes, it's a cheery musical ditty about alcoholism, wife-murder, angelic visitation and Satanic retribution, and as such surely deserves a revival by a Gothic-minded folk group. The full lyrics were reprinted in John Ashton's witchcraft compendium from 1896, *The Devil in Britain and America*. Here is how it begins:

> A Wonder strange I shall relate,
> I think the like was never shown,
> In Westmoreland in Tredenton,
> Of such a thing was never known.

Extensive trawling through old gazetteers has not turned up any placename similar to Tredenton – there are a number of 'Denton' names but these are all in the former Cumberland, not Westmorland. I am therefore unable to say where this ballad is supposedly set. The song tells us that Gabriel Harding was a rich landlord, with rents reaching £500 a year (around £40,000 in current terms). But he was rapacious, cruel, a frequenter of prostitutes and a drunkard, and on the fateful night in question he killed his wife in an alcohol-fuelled rage. When he denied the deed, his angry neighbours resolved to send for the coroner. But, at that moment, an unusual guest arrived:

> His eyes like to the Stars did shine,
> He was clothed in a bright grass green,
> His cheeks were of a crimson red.
> For such a man was seldome seen.
>
> Unto the people then he spoke,
> Mark well these words which I shall say,
> For no Coroner shall you send,
> I'm Judge and Jury here this day.

Having listed Harding's litany of crimes – which also included fleecing the poor – the unnamed supernatural stranger announced that all present were under his protection, before opening the door to an even more unexpected visitor:

> Then in the Room the Devil appear'd,
> Like a brave Gentleman did stand,
> Satan (quoth he that was the Judge)
> Do no more than thou hast command.
>
> The Devil then he straight laid hold
> On him that had murdered his wife,
> His neck in Sunder then he broke,
> And thus did end his wretched life.

A view of the Devil as a tall but otherwise human figure, surrounded by witches and uncanny creatures (owl, raven and cat). (From *The Devil in Britain and America*)

The Devil, having completed his executioner's task, promptly left, his departure accompanied by 'sweet music' from an unknown source. The Judge then also took his leave, and as the dazed populace returned to their homes, they commented that the man clothed in green must surely have been an angel.

After the verses conclude, the document rounds off with 'The Names of some of the chiefest men that live in the Parish,' these being the gentlemen who wanted to preserve the episode in print: Christopher Rawly, Esquire; James Fish, Gent; William Lisle, Gent; Simon Pierce; Ambrose Whir; Oliver Craft; Robert Ford; Thomas Clifford, Yeomen; George Crawly; Peter Vaux; Philip Cook; Francis Martin; George Horton; and Abraham Miles, Husbandmen.

Nothing is known about the circumstances leading up to the London publication of this pamphlet, but I have a few suspicions. It seems possible that an unpopular, miserly landlord did indeed murder his wife, and then had to be restrained by his neighbours. Perhaps during the mêlée the violently drunk man ended up with a broken neck. No one wanted to be accused of murder, so a story was invented for the coroner – a story involving the intervention of a Solomon-like angel, who, as Heaven has power over Hell, commanded Satan to carry out a divinely-authorised execution. Not only does it explain the dead man, but it is also theologically respectable. Perhaps the list of 'the chiefest men that live in the Parish' included those who were responsible for the accidental snapping of Gilbert Harding's neck.

But there's also something else. The Judge, whom the people regard as an angel, is explicitly stated to be dressed in bright green. And then, entirely without purpose for the story, delightful music is heard, music that 'ravisht the hearts of those stood by.' Both these factors clearly indicate that this preternatural being was not an angel, but a fairy. Note, also, that Satan is not described – there are none of the typical demonic indicators, such as horns, cloven feet or the whiff of brimstone. Perhaps the 'Devil' was actually another fairy? Could the Judge have been a member of the Seelie Court (the fairies of light) and the Executioner his opposite number in the Unseelie Court?

All this is of course speculation. We have no historical information, just a small, intriguing and bizarre publication from the 1660s. If ever there was a marker that demonstrates the adage that the past is a foreign country, then surely 'Strange and True News from Westmoreland' is it.

WITCHCRAFT AND MAGIC IN THE EIGHTEENTH CENTURY

In 1735 witchcraft ceased to be a crime in England, Wales and Scotland. This of course did not mean that people in country areas stopped performing the various kinds of folk magic such as divination, healing and hexing, nor did it suggest that the belief in witchcraft ceased – but, given that imprisonment and execution was no longer on the cards, it did bring about a sea-change in the lives of cunning-men and conjure-women. Once the change in law had percolated through society, practitioners of various kinds of magic found it was now possible to earn a living – or at least supplement their income – by developing a reputation within their local area.

One such individual was William Farrar or Fairer, who died at the age of seventy-five in the south Cumbrian village of Orton in 1756. The little we know of him comes from an article published almost fifty years later, in Volume 15 of the *Monthly Magazine and British Register* for 1803. Dr Farrar, as he was known, may have been a genuine medical doctor, or at least he may have passed himself off as one. The article describes Fairer as an anti-conjuror who specialised in de-witching bewitched animals and people:

> If a farmer happened to lose his cattle it was necessary to purify the walls of the house with water sprinkled by this famous conjuror; and in endeavouring to account for the latent cause of this disaster, he generally found small parcels of heterogeneous matter deposited in the walls and consisting of the legs of mice and the wings of bats; which he affirmed to be the work of witches.

Farrar was also called in when people suffered disease or mental illness – for, as in previous centuries, many people held the unassailable belief that such calamities were supernatural in origin. He also performed divination – finding lost things or predicting the future – and practiced love magic on request from spurned paramours or neglected wives. The writer of the article noted, rather sourly, that Farrar made a healthy living from his skills, 'By the power of his occult sciences he attracted gold from the pocket of his customers and by this mean contrived to acquire for himself and his family'.

Genesis *Chap. 1. Ver. 14*   *Prov. 3 Verse 1*   Psalms *19 Ver. 2*   Job *38 Ver. 31*

The kind of image that might have appeared in Dr Farrar's 'Book of Black Art'. (From Ebenezer Sibly, *Astrology*, 1806)

There is an entire stratum of British magical traditions that centre on supposedly adept or mystical individuals who were in fact merely ambitious intellectuals whose education surpassed those of their fellows. Farrar may have been one such, because in Jeremiah Sullivan's *Cumberland and Westmorland, Ancient and Modern*, written in 1857, references are made to Dr Farrar's 'Book of Black Art': 'until very lately it was believed there was great danger in opening this book'. As it happens this allegedly fearful work was no medieval grimoire, filled with incantations for the raising of demons, but a treatise on astronomy and astrology. In a largely non-literate culture, however, books became indicators of unlawful learning, and a man who owned any book other than the Bible was immediately suspect, so perhaps some people did genuinely believe that William Farrar dealt in black magic. Some cunning-men kept a book on their shelves to impress their clients – often the cunning-man could not read himself, but to illiterate country people the simple fact that he owned a book was a guarantee of his power. We can imagine the good folk of Orton being suitably awestruck when Dr Farrar opened his dread book filled with incomprehensible diagrams of the heavenly spheres.

Dr Farrar's table-tomb still stands in Orton churchyard. As the years passed after his death, Farrar's reputation, in common with many other magical practitioners, became greatly exaggerated, so that by 1887 poet Thomas Gibson could tell a tale of a veritable wizard:

> For just across the Lune's broad stream
> A man once lived could solve a dream
> Or by the stars could fortunes tell;
> Circumvent a witch;
> Love philters sell;
> Old Dr Farrar's bones amongst us lie,
> Who read black art, which others mystify,
> Malevolent spirits held in check,
> And laid them low in nearest beck.

Not all magic users were as benign as the good doctor. When Margaret Teasdale died in Gilsland in 1777, a cupboard in her house was found to open onto a secret stairway – and within the confined space were stored the skeleton of a child and the bones of the hand of an adult. The skeleton is, of course, deeply suspicious – was it simple murder or was the child's corpse used for some kind of sinister magical purpose? – but it is the hand that is *prima facie* evidence for witchcraft. The severed hand of a hanged man was a powerful charm known as the Hand of Glory. For best results it was removed while the corpse was still hanging on the gallows, and then pickled in salt and saltpetre and heated in an oven with the herb vervain. Either the entire hand was dipped in wax and wicks inserted into the fingers to act as candles, or fat was collected from the hanged man and shaped into candles that were placed between the stiff, upright fingers. One of the purposes of the Hand of Glory was to induce magical sleep upon everyone in a household, thus leaving the way open for burglars. William Henderson's *Folklore of the Northern Counties of England and the Borders* (1879) records an episode of this practice from Stainmore, just over the Northumberland border from Gilsland. Sometime between 1790 and 1800, a gang of thieves used a Hand of Glory to try and rob the Old Spital Inn. An alert servant girl remained awake and managed to douse the candles with skimmed milk, thus waking the family from their enchanted sleep and causing the villains to retreat. The tale was told to Henderson as absolutely true by the daughter of the servant maid.

As for Margaret Teasdale, her posthumous reputation has been somewhat clouded by Sir Walter Scott's reworking of her as Tib Mumps/Meg O'Mumps, the devious and thieving landlady of Mumps Hall in his novel *Guy Mannering* (published in 1815). This aside, the Teasdales appear to have had a justified reputation for law-breaking, such as obstructing excise men and using violence, and the discovery of the secret cache of bones does strongly suggest that Margaret was involved in dark witchcraft.

WITCHCRAFT AND MAGIC IN THE NINETEENTH CENTURY

Changes in society and education saw the gradual erosion of belief in witchcraft in the 1800s – or at least, when asked, people *said* they no longer believed in it – and by the latter half of the century the subject was receiving interest from a new group of observers. The folklorists and local historians of the Victorian era were often the first people to write down the folk memories of ordinary people concerning the 'witches' of a given district. Thanks to these early pioneers we have records of nineteenth-century magical beliefs and practices, such as these examples from Thomas Gibson's *Legends and Historical Notes on Places of North Westmoreland,* written in 1885:

Countercharms

We were acquainted with a schoolmaster who roasted the heart of a chicken stuck full of pins, with fastened doors, at midnight, and he vowed that the witch came to the door and pitifully entreated him to desist, and promised she would not molest him again. Her offence was that she had bewitched a calf, so that it died, and the schoolmaster (no fool, either, in other matters) thoroughly believed it.

Apotropaic customs

There resided at the village of Winton an old man whose belief was so thorough in witches, that he returned from going to Appleby market because the wheels of his cart came off, never dreaming that it was possible, as was the fact, that the linch-pins had been taken out by the scholars at the boarding-school. This old man used to carry with him a rowan-tree staff, which he forgot that morning hence the mishap. He used to wear in his beaver hat a hare's foot on one side, and a piece of rowan-tree bark or leaf on the other – this, of course, to keep the witches away.

Witch-bottles

It was told to us by Joe Steel, the mason poet, that while digging an ashpit in a house not far from the Wath in Ravenstonedale, belonging to Squire Thompson, he found a bottle full of crooked pins, which he conjectured had been buried to keep the witches away, as he was informed that the children had been ill with a fever, and the cows had cast their calves.

William Henderson's *Folklore of the Northern Counties of England and the Borders,* which came out six years earlier, related the tale of Billy Briscoe, a farmer from Bothal whose relationship with his wife had deteriorated to the point that he paid a wise woman a guinea in exchange for a charm to protect him from his spouse's evil eye. The conjure-woman handed over two pieces of paper, each about three inches square and closely covered with writing (sadly we are given no details about this script). One piece was to be sewn inside his waistcoat, and the other fastened inside the cupboard door. All was harmony for a few months until the waistcoat was washed and the cupboard door cleaned bare, and with both parts of the spell destroyed, the couple resorted to their usual internecine squabbling.

Cumbriana, William Dickinson's book from 1876, includes a first-hand account given to the author by a small farmer from Graysouthen, near Cockermouth. After suffering the loss of four pigs and three cows in just a few weeks, the man suspected witchcraft was afoot. One morning he opened the cow byre and a hare sprang out, leading him to the conclusion that a shapeshifting witch was wreaking havoc among his livestock. He immediately marched next door and dragged the wife of his neighbour Paddy Core into the byre, where he told her he knew she was the hare and that if she did not break the charm he would kill her on the spot. After protesting her innocence and receiving more threats the wizened old woman muttered a few unintelligible words, and said the spell was broken. The farmer let her go, and no more of his animals died. Several decades later, he told Dickinson that he was still convinced that Paddy Core's wife had been a true witch, and that his threats to her had saved his livelihood.

Folklorists have also left us records of three women who in their lifetimes were regarded as veritable witches – Mary Baynes of Tebay, Lizzie Baty of Brampton, and Bett Chambers of Workington. Their stories show us that, in the culturally conservative rural areas, attitudes towards healing and hexing remained unchanged for centuries.

Mary Baynes died in 1811 at the age of ninety but her posthumous fame had to wait until 1885, when Thomas Gibson published *Legends and Historical Notes on Places of North Westmoreland*. This is all that he wrote on the topic:

> A legend occurs that an old woman who resided at Tebay could turn herself into the form of a hare, and in this state used to give sport and much trouble to the dogs of a neighbouring squire, who could never catch her. This old dame prophesied that carriages without horses would run over Loups Fell since verified by the formation of the Lancaster and Carlisle Railway.

We thus have shape-shifting (into a hare) and prophetic declarations, both traditional characteristics of a witch. In 1896, Anthony Whitehead included the transfiguration from human to hare and back again in his *Legends of Westmorland, and other Poems*, but ramped up the list of the witch's accomplishments. According to him, the 'Witch a' Tebay' was excessively ugly, with a hooked nose, toothless mouth and a chin set about with dark hairs. Passers-by smelt brimstone coming from her house and saw a jet-black cat which was doubtless her familiar. It was thoroughly believed in the neighbourhood that she romped around midnight churchyards with the Devil, to whom she had sold her soul. She raised storms to blast crops and brought sickness to man and beast. All in all she was a bad lot.

According to Whitehead's poem Mary Beaynes, as he named her, came to a sticky end because she cast a spell on some eggs, causing the chicks to be trapped inside the shells without hatching. A local woman knew a countercharm involving rowan wood and magpie wings, and cooked the bewitched eggs in a frying pan. Almost immediately Mary was banging on the locked door crying in agony for them to stop, but her neighbours were resolute and as the eggs were burned, a great storm arose and carried the witch off to Hell.

Here are Whithead's notes to his poem:

The hunt described in the poem is currently believed to have taken place, the old witch having turned herself into a hare. Her death is also believed to have been caused by the roasting of some eggs which she had witched; her charm over the eggs had been such, that if destroyed, the witch would then die the same death; this the good dame having found out, roasted them, and thus destroyed old Mary, she was found dead in bed one morning, and upon examination it was found she had died from erysipelas, which had run up one side to her head — of course this was the scorching caused by the frying of the witched eggs.

Three years after Whithead's book came out, Daniel Scott published *Bygone Cumberland and Westmorland*, which cemented Mary's reputation and, as well as confirming her repulsive demeanour and tendency to bewitch people and livestock, also provided the most quoted of all of the old woman's actions:

Many strange things that happened were laid at her charge and thoroughly believed by the people. Ned Nisson, of the Cross Keys Inn had a mastiff which worried Mary's favourite cat. The owner decided to have the cat respectably buried in her garden and a man named Willan dug a grave for it. Old Mary handed an open book and pointed to something he was to read, but Willan, not thinking it worth while to read anything over the cat, took pussy by the leg and said:

Ashes to ashes, dust to dust
Here's a hole and in tha must

A clichéd image showing what witches like Mary Baynes might have got up to. (From *The Devil in Britain and America*)

Mary grew angry and warned her companion he would fare no better than his levity. Soon afterwards Willan was ploughing his field when the implement suddenly bound up and the handle struck one of his eyes causing blindness. Mary Baines was given credit for having bewitched his plough.

With this powerhouse of nasty witchery in print, Mary Baynes became perhaps Cumbria's most famous witch. And yet I have my doubts about how much of the legend can actually be laid at her door. The three Victorian writers quoted above were working seventy or ninety years after Mary's death, and so were unlikely to have spoken to any of the Tebay villagers who had actually known her. If the best part of a century has passed, that's plenty of time for the folklore machine to get into gear. Most of Whitehead's poem is the bog-standard 'witch sells her soul to Satan and regrets it' malarkey, a collection of clichés and stereotypes, but even if Mary Baynes had something of a reputation for folk magic, and may well have had an appearance that conformed to the classic witch physiognomy, I contend that she may have been a much more minor player than her current profile suggests. I put it to you, gentle reader, that she has been much maligned by Gibson, Whitehead and Scott, and by their anonymous tale-tellers from the Tebay area.

We have more reliable sources for Lizzie Baty, the so-called 'Witch of Brampton', who died in 1817 at the age of eighty-eight. She first appears in print in 1843, when Thomas Wilson described her as a fortune-teller in *The Pitman's Pay, and other Poems*. Her speciality was 'recovering things stolen or strayed' and giving lovelorn young women hints about the names of their future husbands – hints, which, Wilson maintained, had been skilfully squeezed from the girls themselves by Lizzie's subtle questioning. She seems to have employed what critics of modern psychics term 'hot reading' – getting the customer to tell you, without them realising it, what they already want. Wilson also criticised Lizzie for taking money in exchange for dodgy advice, and was particularly scathing about her counter charms:

> She was once applied to for assistance in the case of some cattle that were 'dwining away' under the power of witchcraft. She was rather puzzled how to act in this matter; but, after applying her fertile mind to it for some time, she came to the sage conclusion that slitting their tails, and putting pieces of rowan-tree into the opening, would free them from the power that was destroying them. This, of course, was tried; but the owners of the cattle declared that it had no effect upon the disease, and that they might as well have 'laid salt on their tails.' Lizzy, no doubt, often missed her mark on these occasions; but she sometimes made a lucky hit, which kept her fame afloat with the dupes that consulted her.

Wilson's unflattering portrait concluded with a note that Lizzie's daughter had succeeded her deceased mother as the local wise-woman. This daughter is named as Mrs Salkeld in the partial biography of Lizzie included in her next appearance in print, Peter Burn's *English Border Ballads*, published in 1877. Burn had spoken to several people who had known Lizzie, including her next-door neighbour, Mrs Tinling. According to the old woman, Lizzie was born and brought up at Castle Douglas, in Galloway, and eloped with the schoolmaster, John Baty, in the traditional manner (tying sheets to her bedposts and clambering down the outside wall into the arms of her lover standing on the snow-covered ground below). The couple moved to Bewcastle on the Cumberland/Scotland border before settling in Brampton. John Baty was said to have briefly attempted to earn a living as a 'fortune-teller' at Bewcastle, and it is possible that it was this that prompted Lizzie to try supporting herself in a similar manner, a profession she successfully pursued for many years. She habitually wore a red cloak, trimmed with white fur and a full hood, carried a walking cane, and perhaps consciously 'acted the part' of a woman who knew secret and magical things. Mrs Tinling asserted that Lizzie often read the Bible but never went to church, and was a good and kind neighbour who often helped out when the need arose.

Peter Burn went on to give several stories that were told about Lizzie's exploits, which were clearly meant to show that her supporters believed she had genuine powers – none of Thomas Wilson's scepticism here. A Mrs L., accompanied by Mrs Tinling, consulted Lizzie about some lost butter and mutton, and wanted to know the identity of the thief. Lizzie told Mrs L. that the culprit was a spaniel belonging to a Captain Oliver; and that she would find part of the leg of mutton – plus a bar of soap taken by the same dog – in a midden in the Brewery field. Subsequent investigation uncovered the items just as Lizzie had said. When a teenager, Mrs Tinling and a friend went to Lizzie to have their fortunes told – or rather, their fortunes told in respect of love and marriage. Mrs Tinling's friend had been talking of having a white dress for her wedding day, but even before the consultation began, Lizzie blurted out that she shouldn't concern herself with a sweetheart, as she would have a white dress soon enough. A few days later the true meaning of the witch's words were revealed, when the young woman died of a fever, and was buried in coffin clothes of white linen. And a carter, who wanted to deliver

The gravestone of John and Lizzie Baty
in Brampton, photographed around 1960.
(Courtesy of Jim Templeton)

his best coals to another customer, found that his horse refused to move from outside Lizzie's front door. Only after he had unloaded the best stock into Lizzie's coal shed did the horse consent to obey its master (causing horses or oxen to 'stick' was a well-known skill of witches).

On a more sinister level, Burn repeated two stories told of Lizzie that demonstrated how unwise it was to cross a witch. A pair of young girls mocked Lizzie when the frail old woman was knocked down by a running lamb. Lizzie apparently said, 'Ye shall hae laughin' an' dancin' enough efter this,' and when the girls returned home to Hemble's Gate, (also known as Hemel's Yett) they found themselves unable to stop dancing for days on end. Eventually the girls' family made a series of propitiatory gifts to Lizzie, and the charm was lifted. Much nastier was the tale of Mrs G., a farmer's wife from the Carlisle area, who blamed Lizzie for a series of domestic problems – the death of her horse, spoiling of her butter in the churn, and the breaking of bowls holding cream. Mrs G. therefore travelled to Brampton and, without warning, attacked Lizzie with a darning needle, wounding her on the brow. One neighbour, Mrs Rutherford, witnessed the assault, while Mrs Tinling bandaged the wound and helped the shocked Lizzie recover, and both attested to the truth of the event. Thus having blooded the witch – a practice that we also found with Elizabeth Howe more than three centuries earlier – Mrs G. was convinced that Lizzie's curse was now broken. According to Burn, however, the farmer's wife shortly afterwards drowned herself in a well.

We saw with the legend of Mary Baynes that storms often mark the death of a witch. On the day that Lizzie was buried, in March 1817, the traditional weather markers duly appeared, along with other uncanny events, as recorded by Burn:

> Darkness came so suddenly upon the town that lanterns had to be used at the grave, and owing to the high wind the candles had to be re-lighted several times. A singular occurrence took place. A young man named Pickering, either driven by curiosity or overcome by fear, approached too near the grave, and accidentally slipped his foot and fell in.

On 10 December 2010, the *Cumberland News* published an article with the wonderful title of 'Cumbrian Witch's Cursed Tea Set Promises Disaster for New Owners'. It told the story of Lizzie's china tea set, bequeathed to neighbour John Parker on her deathbed – but it was a gift bound by a spell. Any member of the Parker family who drank from the cups would be the recipient of good luck. But if the set ever left the family it would bring trouble and hardship to the new owners. The china set, still in mint condition, was now guarded by a descendent in Carlisle. Jim Templeton – the same chap who took the photograph of the 'Solway Spaceman' (*see* Chapter Seven) – described the family folklore concerning the tea set. Just before he left for service in the Second World War, Jim's mother Mary – who was John Parker's great niece – sent her son to Brampton to drink a cup of tea from the china, so that he would be blessed with luck in the fighting. As it turned out, of the 500 men in his unit, Jim was one of only thirty-seven who returned home. 'I would get these feelings as if I were being prompted to move,' said Jim of his experience of combat in Italy. 'So I did. And then something would land on the place I had been standing – a shell.' Even so, Jim was uncomfortable with the idea of being the tea set's guardian, so it was being looked after by another member of the extended family.

Compared to Mary Baynes and Lizzie Baty, we know far less about the third woman in our Victorian triumvirate, Bett Chambers, the 'Witch of Workington'. The only record of her appears in the *West Cumberland News* for 27 June 1931, and may be a tad inaccurate considering that Bett died in 1839. According to the article, she was originally from the Cockermouth area, and after a life with the gypsies settled in Workington to earn a living from witchcraft. In old age she foretold her own death, predicting that 'when everything went strange' and a great wind came, then her end was nigh. The very next day a storm blew through Workington and several curious neighbours visited Bett's cabin, to find the old witch not merely dead but dressed in a shroud and laid out for burial – by hands unknown.

Lizzie Baty's tea set, around 1960. (Courtesy of Jim Templeton)

WITCHCRAFT IN THE TWENTIETH CENTURY

In 1939, a young woman from London came to an unspecified location in Cumbria to do her bit for the war effort by working on a farm. One evening, the conversation with the middle-aged couple who ran the farm turned to the subject of reincarnation. The girl, who had lost her Christian faith at an early age in connection with the death of her beloved cat, and who had since developed an interest in folklore and mythology, told them she was a believer in the transmigration of souls between bodies, as part of the cycle of eternal return. Encouraged by this statement of what was a most unorthodox belief at the time, the couple revealed that they were hereditary witches, part of a long line of country people who quietly, but not secretly, practised the 'Cumbrian tradition' of witchcraft. After some time passed, they offered to initiate the city girl in the ways of their craft, and so in 1941 Eleanor 'Ray' Bone became a witch. It was the first step in an extraordinary magical life.

After the war Ray Bone returned to London, married, found a house in Streatham, got a job as a matron in a home for the elderly, and continued with her magical practices. Little is known of how the Cumbrian tradition was practiced, but it was probably 'low' or 'country' witchcraft, a mixture of healing, protection spells and divination – something that would have been very familiar to the cunning-men and conjure-women of earlier times in rural Cumberland and Westmorland. In the mid-1950s, Ray Bone was introduced to Gerald Gardner, an eccentric character who was often in the news because he was promoting his own more ceremonial version of witchcraft known as Wicca (later, after the various splits that characterised the fissiparous world of British witches in the 1960s, Gardner's teachings were known as Gardnerian Witchcraft, to distinguish it from other branches invented around the same time). Bone was initiated into one of Gardner's London covens, and via the hierarchical structure of the Gardnerian craft, eventually became the High Priestess of her own coven. Many of the people she initiated there went on to become prominent within the burgeoning world of witchcraft. At the same time, Ray Bone became the *de facto* press relations officer for Gardnerian witchcraft, and in the early 1960s she frequently appeared in the media, doing her best to dispel myths about black magic, sacrifices, orgies and the rest of the blood-and-sex gallimaufry that most people came up with when the word 'witchcraft' was mentioned.

To give an illustration of how well-known she became, in October 1963 she was interviewed by Hunter Davies for the *Sunday Times*, in 1964 she featured in the popular gossip/chat magazine *Tit-Bits*, the *Sunday Telegraph*, and the American periodical *Life*, and in May 1965 she was in the *Daily Telegraph*, this time in a feature by the great poet and mythologist Robert Graves. In 1966 it was widely reported in the press that the students of the Oxford University Liberal Club had voted her in as an honorary member of their society, in preference to the other candidate, Prime Minister Harold Wilson. Ray Bone told *The Times* on 3 June: 'How thrilling. Poor Mr Wilson. No, I did not cast a spell on him. I had not even a clue that I was a candidate. I am much more excited to have beaten him for straight political reasons. I am a very strong Liberal.' On 31 October and 1 November, the same newspaper further reported that Mrs Bone had attended the Oxford University Hallowe'en party and had led the students of the Liberal Club in a ritual designed to make the Liberal Party leader become Prime Minister. Nudity was not involved, but the bright young things were instructed in chanting and a spell of concentration, imagining Jo Grimond walking up the steps of No. 10 Downing Street. Ray Bone said, 'I cannot guarantee Mr Grimond's chances but I have had a large number of successes with my spells in the past.' In this case her magic was less than efficacious, as the Liberals remained in the political wilderness for decades.

This is just a small selection of Ray Bone's media appearances, most of which were accompanied by photographs of her looking like a thoroughly respectable lower-middle-class matron. She can also be seen in the rather sensationalist documentary film *Witchcraft 70*, dancing naked in a healing ceremony with the rest of a coven.

In 1972, tiring of both London and the internecine politics of ceremonial witchcraft, the sixty-year-old Bone resigned as a High Priestess and moved back to Cumbria, where she returned to the simpler ways of her first magical practices, living her final three decades in the remote village of Garrigill (which may have been near the area where she became a witch in 1941). She ran an old people's home a few miles away near the precipitous market town of Alston, and was well-known as the local witch, garnering a reputation for mild eccentricity. In 1984, she presided over the burial service of her husband Bill, this being the first time that a witch had officiated at a funeral in Britain. Over the years she attained 'veteran' status in the eyes of younger generations of magic users, and by the time she was interviewed for the Occulture Festival in 2001 she was regarded as the Matriarch of British Witchcraft. Eleanor Ray Bone died on 21 September 2001, and was buried alongside her husband in the unconsecrated section of the cemetery at Alston.

CHAPTER THREE

THE CURSING STONE
OF CARLISLE

In Chapter Two we saw how a number of people in seventeenth-century Thursby made the connection between calamities – such as illness and the loss of livestock – and the actions of an unpopular local woman, a chain of events that saw Elizabeth Howe prosecuted for (and acquitted of) witchcraft. There is often an unspoken assumption that we moderns are intellectually more accomplished than our ancestors, and that such rank superstition died out with the end of the witch trials. Yet in 2005 an entire phalanx of Cumbrian residents – including local councillors, churchmen and a host of ordinary people – lined up to make a magical connection between a series of disasters and a so-called 'cursed' stone. Just as we store the relics of our reptile ancestors deep inside the structure of our brains, so, it appeared, just beneath our modern sophistication lurks a world-view that is positively medieval.

The problems all started with the redevelopment of the area around the Tullie House Museum and the castle, an ambitious but controversial Millennium Project that eventually ended up going vastly over budget and splitting public opinion in Carlisle, leading to many political changes locally. The human geography of the area had been torn apart by a 1960s dual carriageway, under which ran an unpleasant underpass. The idea was to create a new underpass between Tullie House and the castle, with the cultural footprint of the museum being extended beyond its exterior wall into the public walkway itself, as represented by what the original brief termed as a 'theatre of objects' with a Border City theme. One of the artists whose proposal for this project was accepted was Gordon Young, a sculptor who had been born and brought up in the area. His submission included a granite floor sandblasted with the surnames of the Border Reivers, and the 'Bishop's Stone', a 2.5m-high 14-ton boulder of Galloway granite inscribed with an extract from an ecclesiastical curse placed upon the Reivers in 1525.

For two centuries, the Reivers had terrorised the 'Debatable Lands' north and south of the Scottish Border. Neither of the governments of England and Scotland had found ways to control these wild marauders, who were not mere outlaws but often members of the prominent semi-aristocratic families of the region. They have bequeathed two words to the English language – 'blackmail' and 'bereaved', both of which tell you an awful lot about the daily Reiver dance. Later writers, often taking the lead of Sir Walter Scott, have sometimes

Carlisle Castle.

The Bishop's Stone in the Millennium Gallery underpass. The names of Reiver families have been sandblasted into the floor. (Artist: Gordon Young. Typography: Why Not Associates. Photography: Rocco Redondo. Courtesy of Andy Altmann)

romanticised the Reivers, softening their sting and claiming that, for example, Scottish Reivers only raided south of the Border, while their English equivalents were equally patriotic. But as George MacDonald Fraser's superb study *The Steel Bonnets*, makes clear, Reivers cared not for nation nor allegiance, and their standard practices of arson, plunder, extortion, enslavement, rape and murder were perpetuated on Scot and Sassenach alike.

The new Millennium Gallery opened in 2001. And then things started to go curse-shaped. On 8 September, the news agency Ananova, followed by the *Daily Telegraph* on 4 November and BBC's Radio 4 and website on 5 November, all reported an attack on the Bishop's Stone written for his parish magazine by the Revd Kevin Davies, the vicar of Scotby and Cotehill with Cumwhinton. 'Clearly, the council holds matters spiritual in such trivial regard,' wrote the vicar. He continued:

> … that it can cheerfully commission the equivalent of a loaded gun and regard it as a tourist attraction… Its spiritual violence will act like a cancer underneath the fabric of society. I don't think anyone in their right mind could argue that this is what Cumbria needs just now. Is it a coincidence that the curse was first bandied about in 1999-2000 and now, in 2001, we find that North Cumbria is the worst affected region in the entire country in the foot-and-mouth crisis? The land retains what is spoken against it and the violence acted upon it. As to the future of the stone and the curse it brings, they need to be broken, both literally and spiritually, for all time.

So, in the Revd Davies' view, the inscription of the 500-year-old curse in the Millennium Gallery was directly responsible for the foot-and-mouth crisis that at the time was turning British skies black with the smoke of vast apocalyptic bonfires of incinerated cattle. Strangely enough, other parts of the country were just as badly affected by the disease, but did not have the benefit of a cursed art object to blame. But it was not just a local vicar who was on the case. The cause went up the Church hierarchy to the Bishop of Carlisle, no less. The Right Revd Graham Dow stated that while he did not believe that the stone actually caused the outbreak of foot-and-mouth, the words of the curse still had 'spiritual power' and required counter-measures, 'Words have power and in as much as the curse wishes evil on people it should be revoked,' he said. 'If it has to stay I would prefer a blessing to offset it. We can't treat it as just a joke. People have differing views about spiritual power and its capacity to do evil, but I am sure that it is a real force.' The Bishop told reporters that he was writing to the Catholic Archbishop of Glasgow – the ecclesiastical descendent of the man who originally placed the curse in 1525 – asking him to visit Carlisle to bless the stone and lift the curse. There is no record that the Glaswegian See responded to this request.

In its original form, the curse consists of more than 1,500 words of vituperation and ire. It condemns those under the malediction to the very pit of Hell. All parts of their body, from the hairs of their head to their buttocks, are named and cursed, and they are cursed in all actions, from standing and riding to sitting and eating. All relatives and servants are cursed, including wives and unborn children, along with all property from houses to horses and from chickens to cabbage-patches. They are cursed with thunder and lightning, holy fire, and the Biblical plagues of Egypt. Their bodies are to be hanged and ripped and torn by dogs, pigs

Another view of the stone that supposedly brought a series of catastrophes down on Carlisle. (Artist: Gordon Young. Typography: Why Not Associates. Photography: Rocco Redondo. Courtesy of Andy Altmann)

and wild beasts. And they are excommunicated from all religious buildings and benefits, and deprived of any possibility of eternal life after death. It is, in fact, one of the great curses of history, rich in detail and uncompromisingly comprehensive in its thrust to damn every aspect of the lives of those affected. While it was dubbed the 'Mother of all Curses' by the press, the malison calls itself the GREAT CURSING, and it is actually an example of a distinct form of collective excommunication known as an Article of Interdiction. In the Middle Ages the Catholic Church could ban entire groups – or even countries – from the grace of the Church's sacraments. For example, in 1209 an aggrieved Pope Innocent III placed an Article of Interdiction on King John and his subjects, effectively excommunicating the whole of England until the row was patched up.

The instigator of the curse was Gavin Dunbar, the Catholic Archbishop of Glasgow (1524-1547). At the time, his vast Diocese of Strathclyde included the Scottish Borders and parts of Cumbria. Fed up with the endless litany of death and destruction laid at the Reivers' door, he caused the curse to be read out in every parish of his jurisdiction and published throughout the Borders. Little good it did, however. Before the Protestant Reformation, most medieval people believed they would go to Hell if they died outside the sacraments of the Church, so the threat of excommunication often brought the direst rebels to heel. The Reivers, however, were made of sterner stuff. Not only did they ignore Dunbar's curse wholesale, but when the Bishop of Durham issued a similar curse of excommunication on the Tynesdale Reivers, they held a mock Communion Mass of their own. Reiving continued as a way of life for another eighty years after Dunbar's 'Monition of Cursing', and it was only when the kingdoms of England and Scotland were united under the figure of James VI of Scotland (I of England) in 1603 that sufficient political and military will was found to crush what was effectively the Border equivalent of a cross between a group of Somali warlords and the Mafia. The holy curse was largely forgotten until it was reprinted verbatim in George MacDonald Fraser's book in 1971.

Such was the background to all the fuss in 2001, which, however, then died down for a few years – only to return with a vengeance in 2005. By this time not only had foot-and-mouth hit the tourist and farming economy, but Carlisle food company Cavaghan & Gray had laid off 600 workers, Rathbone's bakery had burned down, major floods had devastated much of Cumbria – and Carlisle United was relegated from the Football League. Clearly such a list of disasters could not be mere coincidence, so there must be a root cause. And that cause, for quite a few people, was the 'cursed stone of Carlisle' (cue dramatic horror-film chords).

On 25 February 2005 a letter was published in the *Cumberland News*. Headed 'How We Brought The Flood On Ourselves', it explicitly placed the blame for the floods on the cursing stone, and called for the artwork to be destroyed. On 1 March both the *Cumberland News* and the *News & Star* reported that a groundswell of similar sentiments, largely led by a non-mainstream Christian faction, had persuaded Liberal Democrat city councillor Jim Tootle to table a motion for Carlisle City Council to get rid of the stone. Here is the text of the motion:

Since the Millennium Project, there have been several disasters reaching Biblical proportions such as foot and mouth, the flooding and many other incidences of loss or damage. Many groups and individuals warned the council that placing a non-Christian artefact, based on an old curse on local families, would bring ill luck on the city. This has seen to be correct, and I therefore urge that the council support this motion to remove the stone, the physical embodiment of the curse on families in the West March.

In the week leading up to the subsequent vote, the combination of municipal politics and medieval thinking generated a veritable worldwide media frenzy, with the story being covered everywhere from New Zealand to Iran (the latter, which is of course a theocracy where political decisions are subject to the whims of religious authorities, were delighted to be able to report on this inspiring example of western civilisation at its best). The coverage in Germany was more thoughtful, tending to concentrate on issues such as freedom of artistic expression, and the dangers of censorship. Several journalists pointed out that Councillor Tootle's description of Carlisle's 'disasters reaching Biblical proportions' might have seemed a mite parochial when compared to, say, the Indian Ocean earthquake and tsunami of 2004. The stone's sculptor, Gordon Young, compared the motion to destroy or remove the artwork to the actions of the Taliban, who had recently demolished several huge statues of Buddha because they were un-Islamic. 'If I thought my sculpture would have affected one Carlisle United result,' he fumed, 'I would have smashed it myself years ago.' In the London newspapers, the attitude was largely gently mocking in tone, which confirmed the fears of many Cumbrians that Carlisle was fast becoming a laughing-stock for letting superstition be taken seriously.

At the local level, the controversy filled not merely the editorial columns but also the letters pages of the *Cumberland News*, the *News & Star* and other papers. Here is a selection of letter-writers' opinions:

Make the thing the centrepiece of next year's bonfire in Bitts Park, then roll it into the river while red hot and it will shatter.

If there is the faintest possibility of a link between some of these disasters in Carlisle and this piece of rock, I would recommend that we get rid of it.

Let's get behind the councillors and bring Carlisle out of the dark by destroying the cursing stone.

Not every correspondent, however, bought the idea that the Curse of Gavin, having lain ignored for five centuries, had returned to haunt Carlisle:

The only people likely to be hurt by the curse are the Liberal Democrats for allowing Councillor Tootle to make them look ridiculous by submitting such a time-wasting motion to a council which must have more important matters to consider.

Cumbria needs rational solutions; better flood defences and proper animal disease controls for example.

Do those people wanting the stone's removal expect us to believe that the curse has behaved like an unguided missile, hitting the wrong target and arriving almost 500 years late?

In an on-line poll conducted by the *Cumberland News*, 48 per cent of those who responded thought that the stone should be destroyed.

After seven days of argument, counter-argument and intense international media interest, Carlisle City Council finally voted on the motion on 8 March, with squads of television cameras waiting outside for live coverage. After a slightly fraught debate, in which one Christian

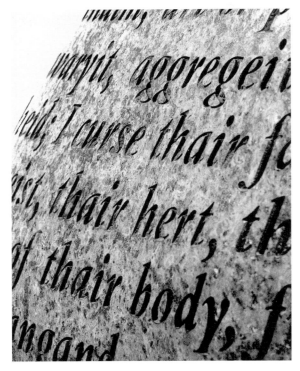

A close-up showing a small extract from Archbishop Dunbar's great curse. (Artist: Gordon Young. Typography: Why Not Associates. Photography: Rocco Redondo. Courtesy of Andy Altmann)

campaigner was ejected for heckling a councillor, the Council voted overwhelmingly to reject the motion. Only Mr Tootle and a fellow Liberal Democrat councillor voted in favour.

The decision did not halt the momentum that the story had now generated. Uri Geller, the astral spoon bender of Sonning-on-Thames, asked to relocate the stone to his garden in Berkshire, where the ley-lines would heal the negative energy. A shaman and healer from Dumfries offered to perform a cleansing ceremony. A white witch wanted to place an anti-curse on top of the stone, while the sculptor Gordon Young received several calls from what he termed 'the nation's cosmic chosen', all suggesting different ways to lift the curse. Another self-styled psychic and astrologer did actually travel to Carlisle with a TV crew to exorcise the stone's negative energy with a circle of salt, a turquoise pendant and a banishing ritual involving her spiritual guides. A Christian campaigner also turned up for the ceremony, denouncing the proceedings as 'witchcraft' and claiming the stone could become a 'shrine for devil worship' (although of course the original curse was pronounced by a senior member of the Christian Church).

With the stone unscathed, however, the heat went out of the debate, and the topic gradually left the front pages. A few London reporters stayed on to write a few last humorous pieces, and the weekly periodicals snickered about how 'it's grimly superstitious up north', but apart from the increase in crowds visiting the Millennium Gallery – and daring each other to touch the 'cursed stone' – the story became yesterday's news. The 'Curse of Carlisle' eventually degenerated into a journalistic joke, so, for example, on 29 March 2005 the *News & Star* reported that BBC *Look North* weather presenter Trai Anfield had been cursed after visiting the stone. And the extent of her misfortunes? She was booked for speeding, she was ill for a week and – surely the last straw – she was late for work when her alarm clock failed to go off. That Archbishop Dunbar certainly knew how to spread fear and terror down the centuries, didn't he? The 'Curse of Carlisle' has by now entered folk shorthand, and everything that goes wrong in the city can be jokingly attributed to the cursing stone.

Meanwhile, back in the seventeenth century, the people of Thursby are blaming their bad luck on the curses of one of their neighbours… *Plus ça change, plus c'est la même chose* (usually translated as 'the more things change, the more they remain the same,' attributed to Jean-Baptiste Alphonse Karr, 1847).

In 2010 a CD of local songwriters and poets, entitled *All Along the Wall,* featured a folk-rock track by Julie Matthews called 'Cursing Stone', where the full story is told in a powerful piano-driven narrative which seems decidedly ambiguous about whether the curse is real or not. And of course the Bishop's Stone still stands proudly in the underpass, outside the wonderful Tullie House Museum which displays many of the thousands of archaeological objects uncovered during the dig for the Millennium Project. Archbishop Dunbar's curse is now far more famous than it was during its first incarnation – see if you can read out some of the words in the original medieval Scots.

Sources: the cursing stone appeared in dozens of publications and websites worldwide in March 2005. In local terms, it was in the *News & Star* (1 March, then every day from 3-10 March, and 14 & 29 March), the *Cumberland News* (25 February, 4, 11, 13 & 18 March) and the *Times & Star* (11 March). London papers included *The Times* (2 March), the *Sunday Times* (6 March), the *Guardian* (9 March), and the *Daily Mail* (3 & 8 March). I am also grateful to Graham Young for sharing some of his experiences via personal communications.

CHAPTER FOUR

POWERS OF THE MIND

PRECOGNITION AND CLAIRVOYANCE

Precognitive experiences are those that seem to show glimpses of the future (and which are then partially or fully verified by the actual turn of events) while clairvoyance can be thought of as obtaining information of events that are happening right now or in the very recent past, but which are either far away or otherwise unknown to the percipient through normal channels. Cumbria's oldest recorded example of clairvoyance is from the year AD 685, when, according to Bede's miracle-filled *Life of St Cuthbert*, written around AD 721, the Anglo-Saxon saint was visiting the Roman ruins at Carlisle when he had a vision of a battle between the Picts and his own people, the Northumbrians. In front of witnesses, including Queen Eormenburh, he groaned as if in pain and muttered, 'Perhaps at this very moment the hazard of the battle is over.' When questioned by the bystanders, he would only say cryptically, 'Do you not see how marvellously disturbed the air is? And who among mortals is sufficient to search out the judgement of God?' Much later, messengers brought news that the Northumbrian army had been soundly defeated at the battle of Nechtanesmere, in Angus, Scotland, and that King Ecgfrith was slain. Cuthbert's vision occurred on the same Saturday afternoon as the battle, 20 May.

The Society for Psychical Research (SPR) was formed in 1882 with the specific purpose of conducting scientific investigations into all aspects of paranormal events, with a specific emphasis on both hauntings and powers of the mind (telepathy, telekinesis, clairvoyance and so on). Still thriving, the Society's archives are a treasure trove for researchers. A particular interest down the years has been precognitive dreams, some of which, although challenging the conventional view of how time flows – that is, we cannot receive information from the future – are nonetheless relatively trivial. For example, the Society's *Journal* from February 1901 contains the case of Guy Ellis, who, the night before a golf match at Silloth in March 1894, dreamed about one of his opponents, and when he woke up gave his golfing partner, Fred Ridley, a precise description of events towards the end of the game:

> We had survived into the final round of the tournament, and one of our opponents on the tee was a remarkable-looking man, previously unknown to me. A big black beard was especially

A stained-glass window in Crosthwaite Church, showing St Cuthbert. (© Geoff Holder)

notable. In the course of the match, soon after the turn (at the 9th hole) I dreamed that it was my honour, and I made a bad tee shot and sliced into a horseshoe-shaped sand bunker, situated on the side of a rise in the ground. My partner, as I gathered from his expression, thought it did not matter much, as we were leading by a lot of holes, and would hardly lose.

On the third day of the tournament, Messrs Ellis and Ridley found themselves in the final, one of their opponents being a Danish man named Brandstaetter who had a full beard that made him resemble the cricketer W.G. Grace. Both men recognised him from Ellis's dream, and when Ellis played a very bad tee shot at the eleventh or twelfth hole, he found it landed in a horseshoe-shaped bunker that he had not seen before. At this point Ridley said, 'Your dream is true, for here is the bunker, and it does not matter whether we win or lose the hole.' As it happened they lost that hole but were so far ahead that they won the tournament anyway. When questioned by the SPR at his home in Newcastle-on-Tyne, Fred Ridley confirmed everything that Guy Ellis stated, except that it was himself who hit the ball into the hitherto unknown bunker, and not his partner. Neither man had visited the Silloth links before, and Brandstaetter had not stayed at their hotel and neither men had encountered him in the tournament prior to the final.

Another strange but minor case comes from *Phantasms of the Living*, a survey conducted by three of the luminaries of the SPR in 1886. W. Walsh, the Bishop of Bedford, described how in 1819 his father, Mr Wybergh How, when a young man, visited his old home at Isel, near Cockermouth, before travelling further south. He had intended to depart with his sister, Christian, on the Monday, but was delayed by an unexpected party. He dashed off a letter to Mrs Forrest, with whom they were intending to stay at Liverpool, apologising for their late arrival. When the brother and sister arrived at Liverpool on Tuesday night, they found that they had travelled faster than the post. Mrs Forrest, however, told them that she knew they were not arriving on Monday because she had dreamed about the party they had attended, and gave specific details of who was there and what they did, down to the precise positioning of a syllabub on an old circular table dragged in from the kitchen at Isel Hall.

Sometimes such precognitive dreams have a more dramatic content. The SPR's *Journal* for June 1978 notes the case of Mrs Kathleen Preston, a retired schoolteacher and amateur folklorist from Kendal. Just before 7 a.m. on 30 November 1977, she dreamed of witnessing a silo-like

Isel Hall. In 1819, a woman in Liverpool had an accurate dream of a party here. (© Geoff Holder)

tower smoking, catching fire and then exploding with such force that ash was spread over the nearby town. Mrs Preston was intensely interested in ESP and other psychic phenomena, and often recorded her dreams in the hope they were precognitive in nature. She immediately sent the dream off to parapsychologist John Beloff – who wrote the subsequent article – and scanned the news media for some correlating event. On 22 December 1977, three weeks after the dream, a grain silo in a suburb of New Orleans caught fire and exploded, killing five people and showering the area with grain dust and debris. Then, on 29 December, a similar grain silo exploded in Galveston, Texas, killing at least twelve people. Reviewing her dream and the news coverage, Mrs Preston thought that although the core elements of her dream – the fire, the exploding tower and the scattering of dust – seemed to be precognitive of one or both of these incidents, in other aspects – how people behaved, where they went, and the nature of the area – the dream was quite inaccurate. She also reported that she had not felt 'present' at the silo, and thought that in her dream she was perhaps watching television coverage of the events, rather than the actual disaster.

Sometime in the 1840s a housekeeper named Elizabeth Gowling, employed at the household of Mr and Mrs Noble in Uckfield, East Sussex, had a distressing dream about a woman in her home area of Bongate in Appleby:

> She had, she said, dreamed that this Bongate woman had gone to a drawer, taken out a piece of rope, proceeded to an outhouse, and hanged herself, and that her daughter had come into the outhouse and cut her mother down.

A week or so later she received a newspaper from Westmorland, which contained an account of the inquest on the Bongate woman; and the manner of her death, along with the discovery and cutting-down of the corpse by the woman's daughter, all corresponded with the dream. Elizabeth Gowling had repeated the dream to three members of the family the morning that it happened, but by the time Mr W. Noble wrote to the SPR about the incident in 1882, the housekeeper had been dead for several years, and Mr Noble could not remember the name of the suicide in Bongate. One of the curiosities of the case is that Elizabeth Gowling only knew the woman by sight, and had never spoken to her in life – so what was the connection that caused her to dream of this relative stranger's death? The episode was recorded in *Phantasms of the Living*.

At 7 a.m. on 8 January 1918 James Saunders, an eighty-four-year-old retired gardener, was lying in bed at his home in Grange-over-Sands when he heard a voice say quite distinctly, 'Tom's coming to-day.' Over breakfast, he told his family that his grandson Tom would be returning from the army in France that day, because he had heard someone say so. They told him he must have been dreaming. Sometime between 9 and 10 a.m Tom walked through the front door. He had sent a telegram telling them that he had been given unexpected leave, but it had not yet been delivered. Although ostensibly precognitive, James Saunders' message may well have been an example of telepathy between Tom and his grandfather. The case can be found in the *Journal* of the SPR for 1919-1920.

On 10 December 2010, in a piece discussing the Templeton family connection to the 'Brampton Witch' Lizzie Baty (*see* Chapter Two), Jim Templeton told the *Cumberland News* that his own mother, Mary, appeared to make an accurate prediction just before her death. She told her husband, 'You will see my coffin three times.' Although dismissed at the time as the ramblings of a very sick woman, the statement was borne out. After Mary was laid to rest in Brampton churchyard, a landslide unearthed the coffin. Then, when the grave was re-made and the coffin re-interred, it was discovered that Mary's uncle had not been placed in the ground beneath her as he should have been. So the grave was re-opened and Mary's coffin appeared above ground for the third time.

CRISIS APPARITIONS

This term refers to incidents where the apparition or wraith of a living person appears when they are close to death. Usually the wraith visits a family member or friend, yet at other times manifests to a relative stranger. Crisis apparitions are difficult to study because they are subjective, spontaneous one-off cases – it is not like going to visit a location where phenomena repeat over time. Researchers are divided as to whether the wraith is actually present in an objective sense, or whether it represents some kind of telepathic communication from the individual close to death.

In one case, which took place between 10 and 11 p.m. some point before 1885, the Revd G.M. Tandy was in his study at Loweswater when, by the light of a candle, he saw in the window his old Cambridge colleague Canon Robinson. Thinking that after a gap of ten years his dear friend had decided to pay him a surprise visit, he rushed outside, but there was no one to be seen. About an hour later, Revd Tandy took the sealed wrapper off a newspaper that he had picked up from a neighbour earlier in the day, and the first piece of news that he read announced the death of Canon Robinson. The account is in *Human Personality and Its Survival of Bodily Death*, written by SPR founder F.W.H. Myers in 1903. The same book records the experience of Hobert Rawlinson, of Cheltenham, who was in his dressing-room one morning when he had the strange conviction that he was not alone – and looking round he had a clear vision of his old friend William Stanley, of Ponsonby Hall (now called Pelham House, near Sellafield). The following day Rawlinson received a letter informing him that William Stanley had died at 8.45 a.m the day before – the exact time of the vision in the dressing-room.

On 25 March 1891, the McAlpine family of Glasgow stayed at the Furness Abbey Hotel in Barrow-in-Furness so as to attend the launch of the large steamship *Empress of China*. Among those joining them for breakfast and lunch was Mr Bryce Douglas, a large, powerfully-built man in robust health. The following day Mr Douglas left to travel on the maiden voyage of another steamer, while the McAlpines remained at the hotel. At 7.50 p.m. on Monday 30 March, Mrs McAlpine passed Bryce Douglas standing in the doorway of his sitting-room, looking at her with a sad expression. Thinking the encounter bizarre, she told her husband and son, and confirming that Mr Douglas was not staying at the hotel, they sent a telegram enquiring after him to his home at Seafield. The following morning they received a reply, 'Mr Bryce Douglas dangerously ill.' He died the following Sunday, on 5 April. Investigation showed that he had been unconscious by the time Mrs McAlpine saw his apparition in the hotel. The case featured in the *Proceedings* of the SPR in 1894.

Around the end of October 1870, Mr A. McDougall was making his regular journey from his farm at Castle Sowerby to his home in Penrith, but was running later than usual because he had taken a meal with the farm labourers to mark the end of harvest. He was at pains to point out that, as he was an abstainer from alcohol, it was a temperance supper. Around 11 p.m. or midnight on a cloudy but moonlit night he passed the Greystoke Pillar about a mile from Penrith.

There, driving slowly as I was about to turn into a narrow lane, I was deeply shadowed from behind, and upon looking back to see what caused the shadow I saw my friend Broome, bending over me with an expression of the most tender affection upon his countenance. I spoke to him, pulled up the horse, and alighted. I walked round the gig, called him by name,

The Greystoke Pillar west of Penrith, where, in 1870, Mr McDougall saw the wraith of Robert Broome at the time of his friend's death. (© Geoff Holder)

begged him not to play tricks at midnight, but to come to me and come home with me. I had, of course, to go without him.

Puzzled, McDougall made his way home. Three days later he received a message that his old friend Robert Broome, from Buxton, had died around midnight on the very night he had seen him near the Greystoke Pillar. This particular episode was written up in the SPR's *Journal* for 1893-94.

As recorded in *Phantasms of the Living*, on Friday, 24 March 1882, three servant girls were sitting in the kitchen of Lindale Parsonage by Grange-over-Sands when they saw a 'ghastly face' at the window. Two of them recognised it as belonging to Mrs Robinson, a former housemaid at the parsonage who had since moved away. The figure seemed to fade away after a while. The following morning, the flower-bed directly by the window was inspected, but no footprints were found. A few days later they learned that Mrs Robinson had died. Following an account provided by the servants' employer, Mrs Willink – who did not see the figure – the SPR became very interested, because this seemed to be an unusual case where a crisis apparition was witnessed by not one but three people. The Society contacted the servants, all of whom had since moved on to other locations. Between 1884 and 1886 each of the women gave a thorough description of what they had experienced. Firstly Mary Jane Farrand (the italics are my own):

> The other two maids, with myself, were sitting at supper in the kitchen, close to the window, when we all became conscious of being watched by a woman from the outside, whom the other two immediately recognised as a person whom they both knew as Mrs Robinson… She looked intently upon each one, and then turned her face quite to the cook, looking slightly reproachful, then pleadingly…One was just about to go and ask her in, when we saw a great change come over the face, and *it looked like that of a corpse*, then disappeared altogether.

Aggy Nicholson (now Mrs Capstick of Carnforth) had a similar recollection:

> We were sitting at supper, and Nell happened to look up at the window, and said someone was looking in, then told us to come and look. *It was like the face of a skeleton*, and we looked, and it was a very thin face, with large staring eyes… It seemed to gradually fade out of sight.

Nell, the cook, wrote from Newby Bridge in 1886:

> Looking at the window I saw, at the side of the blind, which was not hanging quite straight, a very pale face looking at me. It was turned sideways when I first saw it, and thinking it was one of the young men from the village come up to make game of us, I made a face at it; then it turned full face towards me, and I saw that it was the face of Mrs John Robinson … It looked very pale. I watched it with the other servants for about 3 minutes perhaps, and then it dropped down and disappeared. I could see all round it, so that I could see that *it was not a real face*, and it was too close to the window for that. It looked as if resting on the sill.

Mrs Willink and the servants believed that Mrs Robinson had died on the Friday some hours before they saw the figure at the kitchen window. The SPR, however, discovered that she had passed away in Leeds Infirmary the following morning; she was still alive but unconscious when the crisis apparition appeared.

One of the unexplored factors in the case is that, in the intervening years, Nell the cook had become Mrs Helen Robinson, the wife of John Robinson – the widower of the woman whose crisis apparition she had seen. There is an intriguing sentence in the testimony given by Mary Jane Farrand above, when she described how the figure at the window 'turned her face quite to the cook, looking slightly reproachful, then pleadingly.' Was Nell's future relationship with John Robinson a factor behind the appearance at the kitchen window? As the first Mrs Robinson had been ill for a long time, could John and Nell have already been romantically entwined? Was the apparition jealous? Or wishing her replacement well?

DIVINATION

Divination is the process of using mental powers to either glean information about the future, or locate lost or stolen objects. Many techniques are used, from consulting a book at random, especially the Bible (a process known as bibliomancy) to using playing cards (cartomancy), crystal balls or still water (scrying) and a host of other practices. Popular activities such as Tarot cards, the *I Ching* and tea-leaf reading are all versions of the divinatory art.

As with all areas of human endeavour, the paranormal goes through its fads and fashions; automatic writing – where the participant receives information from 'elsewhere' and writes it down, often without understanding the content – was a popular divination tool from the nineteenth century up until the Second World War, but these days has largely fallen out of fashion. In some cases the writer goes into a light trance or an obviously altered state; at other times they can carry out other functions or conversations normally while the 'automatic' hand is scribbling away, apparently unconnected to the rest of the person. Some right-handed people find their automatic writing only comes from the left hand, and vice-versa, while many automatic writers are even asleep while the pen scrawls across the page. Researchers remain uncertain whether automatic writing is somehow accessing parts of the brain that are usually underused, such as memories or deductive capacities, or whether the technique enhances or initiates latent telepathic or clairvoyant capabilities.

One of the more celebrated automatic writers of the late Victorian era was Lady Mabel Howard, of Greystoke Castle west of Penrith. Automatic writing had a certain cachet amongst well-heeled families – it was fun, intriguing and rather elegant, with none of the more vulgar displays associated with séances and mediumship – and so Lady Mabel was encouraged to pursue her talent as a young girl. When she was eighteen, her pencil inscribed the initials of a man who wished to marry one of her friends – much to the friend's disgust, who had asked a question about her matrimonial future, hoping that another young man would be her suitor (many years later, the man with the initials confessed to Lady Mabel that he had set his sights on the girl, but had been rebuffed). On other occasions her automatic writing correctly predicted the date of her sister's engagement – even before the fiancé in question had even appeared in her life – gave the month and year of a friend's engagement and wedding, identified that the tenants of a nearby house had broken a specific table and would therefore have to pay the costs at the end of the lease, and located a book that had gone missing at Sir Harry and Lady Vane's mansion of Hutton-in-the-Forest. All these and many other relatively minor incidents from her automatic writing were witnessed by Lady Mabel's family and aristocratic friends, who

Netherby Hall, near Longtown, in 1909. (From postcard collection of Fowler Beanland under Creative Commons Attribution Share-alike license 2.0)

were more than happy to corroborate her claims when they appeared in the *Proceedings* of the SPR in 1893 and reprinted in *Human Personality and Its Survival of Bodily Death*.

Lady Mabel's greatest 'hit', however, came with her prediction about the discovery of the Netherby Hall jewels. On the evening of 28 October 1885, four men stole a cache of jewellery from Netherby Hall at Longtown, the home of Sir Frederick and Lady Graham. What started as a standard robbery case swiftly escalated into a hue and cry across Cumbria, as the ruthless gang bludgeoned and shot their way through anyone who tried to stop them escaping south by train. Over the next twenty-four hours, they murdered one policeman, shot and wounded two other officers, and beat a fourth unconscious. After several other sightings and encounters, three of the men were spotted sneaking onto a goods train as it departed from Keswick Junction. The guard threw messages for northbound trains passing in the other direction, one of which was picked up by a driver at Shap, and when the goods train made its next scheduled stop at Tebay station, a posse of railwaymen armed with impromptu weapons managed to overpower two of the men (who had been holding revolvers). The third man escaped in the confusion but was later captured at Lancaster station, while the fourth member of the gang, who had departed before the other three, was arrested at Manchester. On 8 February 1886, following a three-day trial in January, Anthony Benjamin Rudge, John Martin and James Baker were hanged at Carlisle. William Baker, who had not been present at the murder of Police Constable Joseph Byrnes, was sentenced to penal servitude. All four had long criminal histories, and Martin had previously murdered a police inspector at Romford, Essex. Tullie House Museum displays a number of gruesome relics from the crime spree, including the skeleton keys and metal jemmy used in the Netherby Hall robbery, a .38 bulldog revolver belonging to John Martin, and a bullet extracted from one of the wounded policemen. The memorial to PC Byrnes can be found on the roadside near Plumpton off the main Carlisle-Penrith road (the A6).

A steam locomotive at Tebay station. The station closed in 1968. (From Ben Brooksbank/geograph.co.uk., under Creative Commons Attribution Share-alike license 2.0)

Although the men were apprehended late on the night of Thursday 29 October, the jewels were not immediately recovered. On Sunday 1 November, with the robbery the only topic of conversation in the area, several of Lady Mabel's friends asked her is she could use her automatic writing talents to locate the missing jewels. Her pencil wrote, 'In the river, under the bridge at Tebay.' This seemed most unlikely at the time, and so the insight was not taken further.

Several days later the first part of the haul was located near Tebay station, close to the river. Some weeks later the last jewels were recovered under a railway arch at Tebay. They had either been thrown onto their find-spots just prior to the struggle, or been lost when James Baker swam across the river while escaping from Tebay and trying to make his way south. Five witnesses confirmed to the SPR that Lady Mabel had correctly identified the location of the jewels while the criminals were in custody but well before the proceeds of their crime had been located.

Another attempt to used mental powers to locate stolen property, this time in the year 1818, was recorded in William Dickinson's book *Cumbriana*. Several farmers from Lamplugh and Arlecdon had lost a number of geese, and so Thomas Fisher, the tenant of North Mosses, decided to consult George Lawson from Egremont, who had the reputation of a seer. Fisher invited a neighbour, Jonathan Boadle, and the young Dickinson along as witnesses, and the three men deliberately set out after dark so as to avoid being seen and mocked for their superstitious errand.

Lawson, a handloom weaver living with a large family in humble circumstances, showed them into a small upstairs bedroom where a globe of dark glass the size of an orange was set on a circular table.

It was now explained to us that the ball was to be held between the two hands of a young person of pure morals and of upright conduct, and closely looked down upon in the dark, and the person holding it would answer questions as to what he saw in the glass, if any discovery was to be made.

Although he was the youngest person present, Dickinson declined to be the operator, and so Lawson's eldest son, a lad of twelve or thirteen, was called in to scry the glass ball. After a few minutes' concentration the boy stated that a dim light was slowly getting brighter in the ball, and his father began to question him:

'And what do you see?'

'Two men catching geese in the corner of a field.

They've got one — they are putting it into a sack — the rest have broke away — they have driven them into the corner again — they have caught two or three more,' he said, hesitatingly.

'Do you know the men?'

'No.'

'What is the field like?'

'A sloping field, and they are in the upper corner.'

At this point the vision faded. After an interval of fifteen minutes the boy said that the light was coming back.

'I see a farmhouse with a tree before it.'

'Only one?'

'One.'

'Do you see the men?'

'No.'

'Do you know the house?'

'No – the light is going – all is dark.'

The description of the farmhouse and tree suggested the residence of a particular local family who had been selling a surprisingly large number of geese at market in recent times, and upon whom suspicion had fallen; but there was obviously nothing conclusive. Dickinson wondered whether Lawson had picked up some gossip about the family and had briefed his son to hint in this direction, but he had no proof. Dickinson also received testimony from Dr Jonathan Langrigg Lawson, who stated that he had generally been sceptical about his brother's supposed gifts until one day the weaver gave him a minutely accurate description of the location of a litter fork missing from his stable. The doctor headed to a certain house in Egremont, where, just as the seer had predicted, he found the stolen tool under the bed in an upstairs room.

LONG RANGE ESP

In June 1975 two very unusual experiments took place in Cumbria. Over the decades some researchers at the Society of Psychical Research, and in parapsychology departments in various universities, had come to the conclusion that Extra-Sensory Perception was real, that is, its effects, whether they involved telepathy, telekinesis, clairvoyance or other actions, could be detected and measured. The obvious question then arose − if, say, telepathy was a genuine ability, how was the 'information' it contained actually transmitted? What was the medium involved? What method of transmission? Several members of the SPR attempted to test the hypothesis that the 'information' travelled by a temporary quasi-material 'path' that linked the sender and recipient in a manner analogous to the way a telephone cable links the person who makes a phone call to the individual who receives it. If this unknown, previously-undetected 'path' (or 'probe' or 'antenna') had some kind of physical properties then, it was reasoned, it would have to obey the laws of physics – so, if the transmission took place over long distances, then there would presumably be a measurable time interval between the signal being 'sent' by one person and 'received' by another.

Thus it was that in 1974 and 1975 several long-range ESP experiments across Britain were set up, sometimes over distances of hundreds of miles. The agent – the person 'transmitting' – would make a pendulum swing at certain specific times, and try to transmit the idea of the pendulum motion to the subject – the person 'receiving' – who also held a pendulum, and would try to pick up the 'message' at the same set time. Both agent and subject had stopwatches calibrated against the BBC time signal. Several of the agents and subjects had previously scored well in ESP tests. The results were summarised by Colin Brookes Smith in Volume 48 of the *Journal* of the SPR, 1975–76.

Of the nine experiments, two took place in Cumbria. On 17 and 18 June 1975, the person acting as the agent drove to fourteen locations on the south coast of the Solway Firth and attempted to communicate with the subject, who was driven to a corresponding fourteen places on the Galloway shore of the Firth. The locations on the Cumbrian side stretched from northeast of Carlisle to Parton near Whitehaven, while the Scottish sites reached as far east as the Mull of Galloway, a full 54 miles across the open Firth from Parton. On the Cumbrian shore the weather was fine, but the subject in Galloway had to battle against rain and strong winds and an overly ambitious timetable. As a result the experiment on the Galloway side was often rushed, which probably had an impact on the accuracy of the recordings.

The day after the Solway Firth experiment the team relocated to the Skiddaw area. Here they wanted to see if a mountain over 3,000ft high had an impact on the transmission of the ESP 'signals' when compared to lower ground. The subject remained in one location – in the Lodore Hotel at the south end of Derwent Water – while the agent motored to two locations. The first, near Bothel on the A591, gave a direct route through the relatively low-lying Bassenthwaite valley to Derwent Water, while the second, seven miles east near Ireby on the B5299, was on the other side of the Skiddaw mountain from Derwent Water. Each location was just over thirteen crow-flying miles from the hotel. For the agent, once again, the weather was clement, while the subject was glad to be sitting in a hotel protected from high winds and heavy rain.

The results were intriguing rather than definitive. It seemed that there was a measurable time delay between the agent transmitting the ESP signal with his mind and the subject receiving it. The article claimed that data across all nine experiments showed that the theorised ESP signal – whatever its actual nature – seemed to travel at between three and five miles per second. So if the 'sender' and 'receiver' were twenty miles apart, the signal might take between four and seven seconds to travel from one to the other. Transmission speeds seemed to be affected by bad weather, especially strong winds – could the 'probe' or 'antenna' between sender and receiver be literally blown 'off course', so that it took longer to find its intended destination? In addition the route over Skiddaw took about half a second longer than that along the low-level Bassenthwaite range. The experimenters were surprised how small this difference was, but

Derwent Water, looking north to the Bassenthwaite valley, with the Skiddaw *massif* to the right.

speculated that thick woodlands – such as are encountered between Bothel, Bassenthwaite and Derwent Water – may also slow down the 'signal'.

Against these claims for having possibly established the quasi-physical nature of ESP transmissions, must be placed the objections that the recording procedures depended greatly on individual reaction times in pressing the button of the stopwatches – and thus massive inaccuracies could creep into the results. So, for example, was the half second delay over Skiddaw actually genuine, or a recording error? Ultimately these experiments are an interesting failure. No one has yet demonstrated a mechanism for transmissions between minds. Which of course brings us back to the core question: if ESP is a genuinely real phenomenon, how the heck does it work?

CHAPTER FIVE

FAIRIES, NATURE SPIRITS AND OTHER BEINGS

The Genii that haunt the romantic valleys, the hills, woods and rivers of Cumberland, are so mischievous and malevolent in their disposition, so terrific in their aspect, and hostile to the human race, that a person would be thought very regardless of his safety, were he to entrust himself at any late hour of the night in the neighbourhood of their haunts. Though of an aerial nature, these beings often assume, during their nocturnal rambles on our earth, a corporeal form, that the gross optic nerves of poor mortals might be able to take their size, form, and aspect. They are generally taciturn; but when they do break silence, their unearthly cries 'make night hideous.' The benighted peasant no sooner hears them than he discovers the imminence of his danger, and hastens home with precipitated steps, his hair standing on end.

Robert Anderson *Ballads in the Cumberland Dialect, c.* 1840.

Fairies have fallen out of fashion in a catastrophic manner. Stating that you have witnessed a ghost or a UFO is – up to a point – an acceptable admission in modern society. But if you claim to have seen a fairy then most people will find an excuse to quickly depart your company. Fairies are deemed appropriate for distant folklore or stories for young children, but today they have been largely excluded from serious examinations of the supernatural. It is one of the curiosities of paranormal research that many people can seriously entertain the idea that we are being visited by extraterrestrials from distant galaxies, while dismissing out of hand mysterious entities that have been part of earthly belief systems for millennia.

This state of affairs is almost entirely due to the infantilisation of fairies during the Victorian period. Prior to the late nineteenth century, many country people had held the notion of the existence of fairies in a mix of awe and fear, well aware that the capricious and mercurial Little People of the Otherworld could be dangerous neighbours to cross. This was also a time when the word 'fairy' could connote anything from a pixie-like being six inches high to a stolid gnome-type figure standing some three or four feet tall, or even a quasi-demonic entity who loomed over the loftiest of men. As dramatic folkloric episodes of often malevolent fairies devolved into sanitised 'fairy tales' for the Victorian nursery, so too did the size of fairies

A typical Victorian idea of the size and form of fairies. This is Ariel from *A Midsummer Night's Dream*.
(From Charles Knight, *The Works of Shakspeare,* 1873)

Puck and the fairy host of
A Midsummer Night's Dream.
(From Charles Knight, *The Works
of Shakspeare,* 1873)

diminish. If you ask anyone nowadays to describe a fairy, they will inevitably talk about a diminutive Tinkerbell-like being with diaphanous wings. Once fairies were curmudgeonly and terrifying; these days they are widely considered as cute and twee.

All of this means that, outside the world of folklore studies, very few people use the word 'fairy' with any seriousness. Attempts have been made to upgrade proceedings by substituting the terms 'faery' or 'faerie', words with some undoubted antique power; elsewhere, writers have expanded the frame of reference to include terms such as 'elementals' (nature beings, such as earth spirits or storm demons) and 'devas' (a Sanskrit word meaning 'the shining ones', and, via the twentieth-century interest in Eastern religions, usually employed to mean beings with a mystical connection with nature). 'Nature spirits' remains a popular alternative term. Sometimes connections are made with the supernatural *djinn* of Arabian and Indian mythology ('djinn' gives us our word 'genie'). Others favour the word 'elves', a term that can be traced back to the magical writings of the Dark Ages (which is why elves are so abundant in *The Lord of the Rings* and other works by J.R.R. Tolkein, who was a formidable Anglo-Saxon scholar). Some writers, however, contend that fairies and elves are two different kinds of entity, which gives just a hint of the taxonomic problems facing anyone attempting to classify the various types.

All of which serves to introduce the rich fairylore of Cumbria, which, you might be surprised to learn, exists not just in tradition and legend, but also in a skein of recent sightings, some of them quite extraordinary.

FAIRY TRADITIONS

In this section I am concerned with traditional tales of fairies, that is, stories that have been told again and again, but which belong to 'the land of long ago.' Many such fairytales circulate in Cumbria – here are just a few of the less well-known ones.

Until 1872, when a great storm sent much of it crashing into the waves, Fairy Rock, near Saltom Pit, by Whitehaven, was widely celebrated as the location for a supernatural soap opera involving love, sex, jealousy and death. The story appeared in the *Whitehaven News* in 1910 and was excavated from the archives by the same paper on 19 January 2011. The basic version was that the caves around Saltom were well known to be the home of a group of human-sized female fairies who dressed in purest white and delighted in dancing while hovering an inch or two above the grass and flowers. The queen of these beautiful creatures fell in love with Julian Mandeville, a young student at the school at St Bees, which was founded in the sixteenth century and is still thriving. Julian took to visiting his beloved's sea-cave by boat, but the fairy queen warned him he could only arrive on the first night of the new moon, and remain only until the moon was full – any variation could not be tolerated. If the night of his arrival was dark she would light a beacon for him.

This arrangement – with Julian spending two weeks out of every four in the arms of his lover – continued happily for some time, but then the student, stung by a colleague's gossipy remark, became convinced that the strict conditions placed upon him were simply there so the fairy queen could entertain another paramour. He consequently rowed out to the cave before the new moon, to trap his imagined rival – but there was no beacon to guide him, and a great storm smashed his boat against the cliffs of St Bees Head. His body was found at the base of Fairy Rock, and from that day thence the fairies abandoned the area. The site can be passed on the Cumbrian Coastal Way from St Bees to Whitehaven, but the sea is eroding the land, and so

A group of sensuous female fairies, similar to those who supposedly lived near Fairy Rock. (From The Brothers Dalziel, *A Record of Fifty Years' Work,* 1901)

the only marker is a sign that reads 'Fairy Rocks – Danger – Unstable Ground – Keep Away.' Some might say that danger, instability and warnings to keep out are, in respect of Fairyland, simply par for the course.

For example, *A Dictionary of British Folk-Tales in the English Language*, published by Katharine M. Briggs in 1971, includes a Cumbrian story dating from perhaps the 1840s or 1850s, but collected in the 1920s. Two children, Jack and Dick, went to a fairy hill to rescue several humans and animals that had been abducted by the fairies. They knelt and prayed and made the sign of the cross, and then circled round the mound seven times, seven being a well-known magical number. This ritual caused the hill to open and release two little boys and a ewe and her two lambs. On a second visit the brave pair performed a similar ritual, this time only circling the mound three times, which released the final captive, Shepherd Alan. But they had been observed by a greedy man who wished to open the fairy hill to obtain the treasure within. He, however, did not make the sign of the cross, and when his perambulations reached the number thirteen, 'the fairy hill opened, all bright lit, and he ran inside it. Then it closed with a snap, like a trap …'

In his *Tour in Scotland* (1772) the pioneering Thomas Pennant, one of the first people to write a travelogue in this country, described a visit to a horizontal coalmine at Whitehaven:

The immense caverns that lay between the pillars exhibited a most gloomy appearance. I could not help enquiring here after the imaginary inhabitant, the creation of the labourer's fancy, The swart Fairy of the mine; and was seriously answered by a black fellow at my elbow that he really had never met with any, but that his grandfather had found the little implements and tools belonging to this diminutive race of subterraneous spirits.

The remnants of the Fairy Rock at Saltom, near Whitehaven, with a suitable warning regarding Fairyland. (Alan Cleaver)

The swart (dark) fairy was clearly a species of Knocker, an underground spirit well-known to German miners since at least the sixteenth century. In 1952 a survey of fairy belief conducted by L.F. Newman and E.M. Wilson for the journal *Folklore* turned up a tale dating from around 1855, retold by the grandson of the man who related the story many times during his youth:

> There was an old farmer at Lupton called Michael Black. He was coming back one night from Kirkby Lonsdale to Lupton, and when he came to four lane ends on the Kirkby Lonsdale-Lupton road, he found a hedge across the road. A little gentleman came up to him and promised to help him if he gave him a pound of butter off his back. He would make him a road through the hedge. The farmer did, and he eventually got home in the early hours of the morning, minus the pound of butter. And when the son went onto the road next day he found the butter on the wall-top.

In 1900, a Mrs Hodgson gave a talk to the Cumberland and Westmorland Archaeological and Antiquarian Society entitled 'On Some Surviving Fairies'. In it she included information passed on to her by an anonymous witness in an unnamed district of Cumberland. He pointed out a wood where the fairies once dwelt, but the little folk had fled when the trees were cut down. The informant also had a fine folktale:

> There was a fairy that looked like a hare. It was a real fairy, but a man caught it for a hare, and put it in a bag, and thought he would have a nice Sunday dinner. While it was in the bag it saw

its father outside, and he called to it 'Pork, pork!' and it cried out 'Let me go to daddy!' And then the man was angry, and said 'Thoo ga to thy daddy!' and it went away to its daddy; and he was very much disappointed at not getting his Sunday dinner.

Why, one has to ask, was the hare-fairy called 'Pork, pork'?

FAIRY ENCOUNTERS IN THE NINETEENTH CENTURY

In this section we look at cases where people claimed to have had direct encounters with fairies, at a time when increased literacy, and the interest of folklore collectors and intellectual travellers, meant that such episodes were being written down with greater frequency.

On 25 October 1860, Daniel O'Hara was acquitted of handling stolen money because he believed the fairies had brought him the coins. Not only that, but he went on to give detailed descriptions of the fairies' habits – they were little creatures who sat by the fireside in the morning counting their money, before flying up the chimney when disturbed, and they appreciated gifts of milk and tobacco. The background to the trial was the theft of fourteen gold sovereigns (worth around £600 in today's terms) from an old woman in Whitehaven, the thief being the O'Hara's young daughter. When Mr O'Hara queried the welcome influx of new money, his duplicitous wife told him 'the little fairies had likely sent it,' and he thought no more about it. So when the police came calling, he readily described the activities of the family fairies. No hint about his character is given in the report – which resurfaced in the *Whitehaven News* on 13 October 2010 – but Mr O'Hara was found not guilty at the quarter sessions, while his wife was sentenced to twelve months' imprisonment with hard labour.

In 1850 Jack Wilson encountered a group of fairies on Sandwick Rigg, in Martindale. When the little folk spotted him they ran up a kind of ladder into a cloud, pulling the ladder up behind them so that Jack could not follow. The episode appeared in Jeremiah Sullivan's *Cumberland and Westmorland Ancient and Modern*, published in 1857. One of the strangest of the several fairy encounters included in William Dickinson's 1876 book *Cumbriana* concerns a calf seen floating high over the Irish Sea, coming to land on the previously-mentioned Fairy Rock near Whitehaven. When the creature touched down the unnamed witness exclaimed: 'God! weel loppen cofe!' (roughly, 'Well leapt, calf!') and the utterance of the holy name caused the paranormal animal to vanish. According to William Dickinson, this was the 'last fairy to be seen in Whitehaven', but why a flying calf should be equated with a fairy is beyond me. Note that both episodes deal with unusual aerial phenomena, with the Martindale incident involving what could even be a craft; you would not be the first to notice a family resemblance between fairy sightings and reported encounters with UFOs and aliens.

FAIRY ENCOUNTERS IN THE TWENTIETH CENTURY

For this section, it is time to introduce you to one of the most extraordinary figures of twentieth-century British occultism: Geoffrey Hodson, the man who has perhaps encountered more fairies in Cumbria than any other person in the past hundred years. Hodson was born in Lincolnshire in 1886 and after a full life died in New Zealand in 1983. He was a clairvoyant – able to use his 'inner eye' to observe and communicate with otherworldly entities, who are undetectable to most humans (this of course immediately raises suspicions, as none of his reported encounters can be independently verified). He was also an ordained priest in the

Liberal Catholic Church and a leading light in the Theosophical Society. Theosophy (which means 'divine wisdom' or 'god-wisdom') is a mystical doctrine popular in esoteric circles since the late nineteenth century. The exact nature of its teachings seem to vary depending on the viewpoint of the individual Theosophist, but at its core is a notion that all life and energy is linked on a fundamental, spiritual level, and hence humans, although largely spiritually not evolved, can theoretically communicate with various classes of beings, from spirits to angels and deities. The Liberal Catholic Church was founded in 1916 by schismatic Catholics unhappy with Vatican dogma. Because of its openness to ideas such as reincarnation, mysticism and Theosophy, the Liberal Catholic Church is regarded by orthodox Catholics as heretical.

After frontline service in the First World War, Geoffrey Hodson married Jane Carter from Kendal, and the couple settled in Preston. As his clairvoyant faculties increased he took to touring England on a motorcycle and sidecar, dictating to Jane his visions of various kinds of nature spirits. In 1925 the fruits of these field trips were published in *Fairies at Work and Play* – not, according to the title page, *written* by Geoffrey Hodson, but *observed* by him.

Fairies at Work and Play is a truly unusual work – the nearest analogy is to a naturalist's field guide, only here the creatures being described from direct observation are not moles or waterfowl, but gnomes and undines. With its observations on the clothing, habits, intelligence levels and behaviour patterns of fairies, it is a natural successor to the first anthropological work of this kind, *The Secret Commonwealth of Elves, Fauns and Fairies*, written, apparently from first-hand experience, by the Scottish Episcopalian minister the Revd Robert Kirk of Aberfoyle in 1691. Hodson's work, however, specifically links the fairies and their multitude of preternatural cousins to the processes of nature – for, according to him, it is these ethereal beings that power the budding of plants, the birth and growth of animals and humans, and even the very nature of mountains, rivers and the weather. In Hodson's view, there was a spiritual continuity between the lowly pixies beavering away on tree roots and chicken eggs, and the grand angels and archangels who were the guardians of the greater world; indeed, over time the lesser beings could evolve up the mystical food-chain, gaining intelligence and responsibility as they did so.

A great many of Hodson's observations were set in Cumbria. He had a taxonomic system, classifying the various entities by their behaviour, physiognomy and ecology, and I shall follow this pattern here.

Brownies

Hodson regarded brownies as small male entities of very limited intelligence, who commonly appeared dressed as medieval peasants. They enjoyed imitating human forms and behaviours – clothing, house styles, even the shape of being human – even though they did not truly understand what they were copying.

On 28 June 1922, Hodson observed a large colony of brownies in dense woodland of oak, hazel and beech on the western side of Thirlmere. They appeared to have the busy activity and general lack of individuality that characterises an ants' nest. Many tiny thatched wooden houses had been built just below the surface of the hillside, but when Hodson attempted to investigate one of the houses clairvoyantly, he found that they were mere façades, with no interior rooms, for once the brownies passed through the front doors, they transformed into some kind of formless state to descend deeper into the earth. A typical member of this particular

Thirlmere from the north, with Helvellyn on the left. Geoffrey Hodson saw many species of fairies near here.

colony appeared as a stout, wizened, grey-bearded man some six inches tall, wearing boots, a nightcap-shaped brown hat, and a brown suit with stockings and knickerbockers or breeches. Another member of the village approached Hodson, allowing him to notice that this figure was clean-shaven, slimmer, more colourful and far more supple than the typical brownies – Hodson speculated that this may have been a different species altogether, possibly an elf.

In November 1921, an elderly brownie approached Hodson from a firwood facing Helvellyn. He was thinner and slightly taller than the Thirlmere examples, rather more self-aware, and his clothing – coloured with green and fastened with buttons – also seemed superior. He was fascinated with the party's dog, coming nose-to-nose, but it was Hodson's canvas-topped army gum-boots that truly captivated its attention. After some effort, the brownie 'grew' or mentally projected copies of the man's boots over his own previously naked feet. He strutted around in his new footwear for a while, pleased with his fashion-consciousness, and then wandered back into the woodland. This was another episode which convinced Hodson that some fairy beings liked to imitate humans. (After writing this paragraph, I felt compelled to dig out an old piece of music – it was, of course, the heavy metal Black Sabbath classic 'Fairies Wear Boots'.)

Gnomes

To Hodson, gnomes were elderly-looking, solitary and often rather unpleasant earth-spirits or elementals, of a distinctly grotesque appearance. They were always male, and often black or peat-brown in colour. He encountered two very different gnomes somewhere in the Lake District in June 1922. One, which he called a 'domestic gnome', he clairvoyantly saw living under the ground beneath a rock. As with the brownies mentioned above, the gnome's limited faculties had found pleasure in imitating human behaviours, so, when 'at home', he wore a kind of tasselled nightcap and carried a candle, while when 'going out' he sported a tall top hat. He gathered water from the nearby lake in a bucket – although the liquid was entirely insubstantial, 'looking like a wisp of grey smoke or mist in the bucket' – and left Hodson's vision when he travelled swiftly over the lake, moving about two feet above the surface of the water. An utterly different kind of entity was something Hodson described as a 'rock gnome'. This was a kind of *gnome in utero*, an insubstantial form slowly evolving from an etheric embryo into what would eventually be a conscious entity. Hodson described it as a kind of artist's preliminary sketch prior to a full painting. The gnome-in-waiting was centred on a boulder, but being ten to fifteen feet tall, its 'feet' were deep in the ground and its 'head' rose above the rock.

Mannikins

This was a category Hodson used for diminutive male fairies who, in some respects, resembled brownies, elves or gnomes, but had their own distinct identity. They were always associated with plant-life – trees, hedges, grass, wild flowers, heather and bracken – and usually dressed in green, with a happy, smiling, child-like expression. Less intelligent than brownies or elves, they were nevertheless usually intensely curious about humans, approaching closely without fear. Based on his experiences, Hodson contended that mannikins were the most common type of fairy in England.

In December 1922, Hodson observed a clan of mannikins happily pottering about in the undergrowth and fallen leaves of a wood near Kendal. There was no obvious purpose to their movements, although occasionally groups would join together for some kind of game – at one point four mannikins joined hands and danced clockwise for about twenty seconds. The members of the group exhibited a wide range of apparent ages. One very old mannikin sat exhausted at the foot of an ash tree, and as Hodson watched, faded into the trunk, leaving behind a kind of outline of itself, 'just like a fairy ghost.' Ten minutes later, the creature re-emerged from the tree, entirely rejuvenated, and scampered about, attempting to beckon his human observer further into the fairy wood, of which he was immensely proud.

Undines

Undines are beautiful, nude, female spirits of fresh water. In Hodson's estimation they were of a higher evolutionary order than gnomes and brownies, having a conscious understanding of their responsibilities in perpetuating the cycle of nature. In November 1921, the clairvoyant observed two kinds of undine at Dab Ghyll, the waterfall near the southern end of Thirlmere. The first figure was some four feet tall, silvery-white in colour, with a circlet of gold stars around her head. She moved up the fall to the top of the mountain in a series of rapid darting movements, sometimes languidly sinking into and below the rock surfaces, before re-emerging again full of vigour to continue the upwards journey. Hodson sensed that her behaviour was helping power the natural cycles of water and vegetative growth, and that the rocks into which she habitually disappeared had especially high concentrations of fairy energy, 'which has given the place a strongly defined aura and influence of its own.'

This being seemed to supervise a group of five or six smaller undines, each less than a foot high, who inhabited the waterfall where it reached the lake. These spirits continuously sang in joyful high-pitched voices as they rode up the spray, standing upright, arms outstretched, with their heads held back in a kind of ecstasy. When they reached the top of the falls they released the accumulated energy in a vivid outpouring of colours, 'radiating joy and delight in all directions'. These undines also absorbed sunlight, similarly releasing it in an explosion

Two of the waterfalls where Hodson may have seen undines – Lodore Falls near Keswick.

Aira Force at Ullswater.

of light that caused them to lose their shape for a moment or two. Hodson frequently used words like 'delirious' and 'pleasure' when describing the undines' behaviour, and considered this absorption and release of energy essential to the health of the plants and trees in the ghyll. In June 1922, Hodson also observed a flock of nature-spirits skimming over the surface of Thirlmere, their appearance being something between large birds, clouds, and indistinct shapes of white light or energy. The same month, Hodson watched a full-size undine disport in an unnamed Lake District waterfall: unlike the undines previously mentioned, this creature had wings, and radiated a permanent rainbow-like sphere of powerful light. Hodson was clearly entranced: 'She seems to ensoul the rocks, trees, ferns and mosses, as well as the actual waterfall itself…to contact such a creature is an illumination…the place is vibrant with her life.'

Fairies

Hodson applied this term to entities that exhibited the 'traditional' appearance – small, winged, female beings. In December 1922 he observed a group of such fairies near Kendal. They were graceful, gentle creatures, very feminine, with long hair, garlands of tiny lights, and wearing light, filmy garments. In the previous August, the clairvoyant had watched another group of fairies dancing on a small burn-side plateau somewhere in the Lake District. Around six inches high, they were dressed in pale blue and a number were carrying horn-like musical instruments. Their hair was brown, their skin a pale rose-pink, and their wings light blue. They held hands in a ring and then performed a movement similar to the country dance known as the 'Lancers', with linked chains of dancers moving in lines across the circle, all the while surrounded by a dome-like aura of misty silver energy that secluded them from the rest of the world. The net result appeared to be the budding of many small daisy-type flowers, although by the time Hodson lost sight of the group they seemed to be also creating a kind of globe-like building.

Sylphs

Hodson witnessed a large group of these spirits of the air on the slopes of Helvellyn in April 1922. Resembling birds or bats with human faces, over a hundred of them flew energetically in front of approaching storm-clouds, sometimes emitting 'a weird shrieking sound.' Hodson gained the impression that they were 'working up' the storm.

Devas

These higher beings, radiating light and energy, are the very essence of Nature, being responsible for the macro-processes that characterise the natural world – the formation of landscape, birth/germination, development, reproduction, and death and decay. Although Hodson regarded them with awe, he found them truly alien, without sentiment or emotion – in his opinion, 'they would not discriminate between a wrecked human body and a lightning-riven tree.' They represented Nature's point of view, where death was just another part of the cycle of change, and an individual human life had the same value as that of a hedgehog or thorn-tree.

Hodson found that the whole of the Lake District was densely populated with devas. On 26 November 1921 he had seen more than a hundred devas in the Mythburn area near Helvellyn, their robed figures clothed in rich hues of brown, green and yellow. One female deva, larger and more glorious than the rest, stood eight feet tall, with large angel-like wings of red and gold, and, like the others, appeared to be a creature of the upper hills. In June 1922, he

Striding Edge on Helvellyn. Hodson regarded the mountain as the abode of hundreds of nature-devas.

witnessed several nature-devas on a Cumbrian fellside. The majestic figures resembled radiant humans dressed in Greek robes, and surrounded by an aura of immense power and beauty, with vortices of light and energy pouring out from the top of the head, the forehead and temples, the throat, and the solar plexus. The same month, the clairvoyant encountered an even more striking entity somewhere on a Lake District mountain. On first impression, it resembled 'a

A landscape fit for the gods? Here Hodson supposedly witnessed deva who he called 'The God of Helvellyn'.

huge, brilliant crimson, bat-like thing' whose aura of power stretched for several hundred feet, 'with wings outstretched over the mountainside.' It appeared surprised by Hodson's sudden arrival, at which point it instantly shrank to a more human figure a mere ten to twelve feet high. After fixing Hodson with a penetrating, burning glare, the entity sank into the ground and vanished. Hodson was left with an impression of a raw, masculine virility that created and energised the entire surrounding landscape. 'My physical body thrilled for hours afterwards,' he wrote, 'with the force of the contact and the *rapport* established between us.' It was the clearest and most powerful vision he ever had.

As with other spirits, devas were found at Thirlmere, one of Hodson's favourite places in the Lake District. In February 1922, he observed a host or tree-devas within an ancient firwood on the western shores of the lake. The wood itself seemed to have an independent 'ensouling consciousness', with individual trees being cared for by assigned devas who floated at the level of the treetops and served a higher being. The tree-devas appeared to operate on a level of group consciousness, and, being less evolved, appeared as human only at the head and shoulders – and their eyes were supernaturally bright, intent only on their charges and oblivious to anything else. In June of the same year Hodson observed a deva in the form of a beautiful androgynous youth hovering over Thirlmere, its intense gaze concentrated on the very depths of the waters. Hodson, who watched the deva for more than half an hour, had the impression that the entity was working on natural processes at the bottom of the lake.

The God of Helvellyn

This is the phrase used by Hodson to describe a 'super-deva' or angel of immense size who resides near the summit of the Helvellyn *massif*. From a distance of three miles, Hodson's clairvoyant vision perceived the 'god' as a titanic seated human figure, 'motionless and expressionless save that the eyes are ablaze with power – the power of a highly unfolded and awakened consciousness.' The figure's visible aura – consisting of tongues of flame – was a thousand yards across, while its sphere of influence extended throughout its territory, the entire forty miles' circumference of the Helvellyn range.

Elsewhere in *Fairies at Work and Play*, and in its 1927 follow-up, *The Kingdom of Faerie*, Hodson describes encounters with the many kinds of nature-spirits in Lancashire, London, the Cotswolds, the Home Counties, and Switzerland. In later life, he travelled and lectured extensively – reportedly observing fairy-type beings in New Zealand – while writing dozens of books on Theosophy, mysticism, angelology, clairvoyance and other spiritual subjects. Here is a typical example of his work, extracted from the section on fairies in *Angels and the New Race* (1929):

> The various kingdoms of Nature are their field of evolution. We find them in the woods, by the flowers of the meadow and the garden, in water, in air, in fire, in earth, as well as associated with the metals and jewels of the mineral kingdom. Wherever the divine life is manifest, there are God's faerie children, the nature-spirits, and their elder brethren, the angels, who are shining and beautiful embodiments of His life.

In terms of the Cumbrian material, how are we to assess this extraordinary effusion of reports of fairy sightings? As noted above, all of Hodson's clairvoyant observations were entirely subjective and internal, with no else witnessing what he claimed to perceive with his inner eye. This immediately raises suspicions – could he have made the whole thing up, or simply be deluded? To cloud matters further, in 1921 he was one of the investigators in the infamous Cottingley Fairies case, in which two young girls claimed to have taken photographs of fairies near their Yorkshire home. The photographs were widely publicised by Sir Arthur Conan Doyle, and, despite the fact that the fairy images seemed suspiciously like cut-outs, Hodson believed the girls completely, and wrote extensively of his own inner visions of fairies at Cottingley. In the early 1980s Frances Way (*née* Griffiths) and Elsie Hill (*née* Wright), now both old ladies, finally admitted that the photographs were faked, and that they had been stringing Hodson along – indeed, they thought he was a fraud. (For the full story, see Joe Cooper's superb investigation, *The Case of the Cottingley Fairies*, published in 1990.)

On the other hand, Frances Griffiths in particular was adamant that although the images were hoaxed, she had indeed seen fairies in the glen; so is it possible that Hodson's sightings at Cottingley were entirely genuine? The universal view taken by all those who have met Hodson is that he was a sincere, thoughtful, kind, generous and quietly inspiring individual, and there is no hint of delusional fantasies in his make-up. He clearly believed that we were surrounded by legions of nature-spirits, an opinion not powered by mere conviction, but apparently by direct experience. Of course, this does not mean that his observations should be treated without critique: in the end, it is impossible to say whether Geoffrey Hodson genuinely saw fairies or not. But his testimony is certainly one of the most extraordinary around in paranormal research.

As a way of rounding off this section, I mention an episode from *Quicksilver Heritage*, Paul Screeton's 1974 exploration of 'the mystic leys and their heritage of ancient wisdom'. I should point out that personally I am deeply sceptical about alleged ley-lines and their alleged mystical properties – a subject treated in depth in my book *101 Things to Do With a Stone Circle* – but in terms of this story all that is by-the-by. Screeton was following a ley-line from the railway marshalling yard at Kingsmoor along a narrow road into Carlisle when passing traffic obliged him to walk on the grass verge. There he stepped on a quartz stone that had been worked into a convex shape. Quartz has a particular attraction for those interested in earth mysteries, for it is found at a number of prehistoric sites and, if rubbed together, produces small-scale electromagnetic effects known as piezoelectricity. It is often speculated that the peoples of the Neolithic and Bronze Age had a magical or spiritual relationship with quartz. Screeton therefore touched the stone for perhaps thirty seconds, and then continued walking, but had not gone more than a couple of paces before he saw something move about a yard in front of him:

> The thing leapt like a frog and was frog-shaped, but about three feet high. It was brown but its form was hazy, difficult to describe, but the effect was not dissimilar to a television screen when the lines go crazy. I had the impression that what I had seen was an elemental and that I perceived it at the edge of my consciousness.

Screeton considered that what he had seen was one of Geoffrey Hodson's earth gnomes, and gave three possible explanations for his experience: firstly, it was a hallucination; secondly, the energy of the ley-line had somehow rendered the elemental visible; and thirdly, the contact with the quartz stone had changed his perceptions or consciousness so that he had been able to glimpse the elemental.

TWENTY-FIRST CENTURY FAIRIES

On 15 September 2009, the *News & Star* reported that the previous month several fairy-sized houses had appeared among the trees of Gelt Woods, near Brampton. Beautifully constructed and painted, some had names such as Ivy Cottage and Mossy Hows, one had a pair of miniscule green pixie boots outside the front door, and another boasted a sign asking the postman not to deliver junk mail. Then, on 21 September, the inhabitants of the little houses wrote to the newspaper indicating that they were moving on for the winter:

> Now we can smell winter in the air, see it in the browning leaves and feel it in the crisp morning dew, it's time for us to go. We won't forget you and we will return; but until then

A sign that appeared in 2011.
(Author's collection)

One of the twenty or so fairy houses near Gelt Woods. Note the letterbox and pixie boots. (Ségolène Dupuy)

we must cast a spell of invisibility over our homes. We have spent this summer in your hedgerows and would like to thank you all for not disturbing us. The Cumbrian nights have seen magical dances and singing up the winding lane and the soft shine of the moon on the river has guided the revellers home. The green shoots of spring will herald our return. When the last frost melts, and the first swallow appears, our spell will lift.

The next year, on 10 August 2010, the *Cumberland News* reported that the houses had returned, and had even doubled in number to a total of sixteen miniature dwellings – although they were not complete houses as such, more façades (shades of Geoffrey Hodson's imagery of fairies creating house frontages in imitation of human preferences, but simply blending into the roots and soil once beyond the front door). On 24 September 2010, the pixies sent an email to the paper, once again giving notice of moving on:

Dear People of Greenwell,

We have spent another summer in your hedgerows and would like to thank you all for the gifts of flowers, berries, nuts and sticks – and the pencils and a wooden door.
We watched all you big and small people coming to see us.
Some of you were so quiet our lookouts only just warned us in time to hide, and some scared us off with big, wet-nosed dogs.
Some of you looked in our houses – but you couldn't see anything as we cast spells when we go out. Some helped us when the weather damaged our homes and we all thank you for this kindness.
We hope we didn't disturb you with our parties.
There were more of us this year as our friends wanted to see the magical place we told them of during long winter nights.
When spring is in the air we hope to return. Look for us when the last frost melts and the first swallow appears.

We wish you well,
The Pixies and Fairies of Greenwell

The pixies and fairies returned in 2011.

Interestingly enough, the Brampton area has a long history of fairy activity. In 1876, William Dickinson published the tale of 'Jwony and the Fairy' in his book *Cumbriana*. Jwony was a miner who worked at Tindal Fell, southeast of Brampton. One day after work Jwony went to an illicit still to pick up a batch of whisky for himself and his colleagues. Whilst there he had a glass or three of hooch, so by the time he staggered back he was a tad unsteady on his feet, and soon he decided to lay down for a nap beside a stream. Unfortunately he rolled into the beck, and despite the shallow depth at that point, he could not extricate himself. Fortunately he had with him his faithful hound Swan, and the dog set off home to get Jwony's wife Betty. But in the meantime Jwony had a visitor:

A little man, of less than a foot high, dressed in green, and perched on his shoulder; he remained there till Betty came, and then he vanished. Jwony fancied the little creature had the power, and kept him down, and he used to say, 'If it hedn't been for Swan and Betty, I med ha' tofert in t' beck; for it was them 'at freetn't t' laal thing away.'

A fairy front door, window and flowerpot, with a card that reads 'Dear Fairies, we have brought some presents for you. We hope you like them'. (© Geoff Holder)

A fairy house in a dry stone wall, with a rope ladder to gain entry, and one of the many cards and gifts left for the fairies. (Ségolène Dupuy)

'Laal' is Cumbrian dialect for 'little'. According to Dickinson, the old miner told the story and believed in it until his dying day; you, of course, may perhaps suspect that the psychotropic properties of moonshine whisky might have played a role in proceedings.

We finish with a couple of final contemporary references to the ways the Little Folk manifest in our modern world. On 16 July 2008, the *North West Evening Mail* revealed that, according to a survey conducted by a local dental practice, the Tooth Fairy of South Cumbria pays more than anywhere else in Britain – an average of £1.87 per tooth, which is 35 per cent higher when compared to the national norm of £1.22. And on 19 January 2006, the *News & Star* reported the case of a man who set fire to a car… because it was full of goblins. The individual admitted he might have had a drink or two before the incident, which possibly contributed to his belief that the Ford Fiesta was infested with small, supernatural creatures. South Lakeland magistrates passed down a supervision order and ordered the would-be goblin-hunter pay the £500 cost of damage to the car.

CHAPTER SIX

THE MYSTERIOUS MENAGERIE – FROM BIG CATS AND BLACK DOGS TO LAKE MONSTERS AND WEREWOLVES

Cryptozoologists – those who study unknown or out-of-place animals – love Cumbria. Not only are there established, recognised colonies of South American coatimundis and Australian wallabies living in the area, but the county is home to an entire menagerie of mysterious beasts, some of which appear to be flesh-and-blood, while others may be supernatural or folkloric in origin – and one or two may simply exist as little more than publicity stunts …

LAKE MONSTERS

Cumbria is, obviously, a land of lakes. And there is something about large bodies of fresh water, with their unseen inhabitants lurking beneath a reflective surface, that seems to set something off in the murky depths of the human mind. Imagination can populate these waters with all manner of beings, and the legends and mythologies of the world have benefited accordingly. In recent times, many people have become convinced that a number of lakes around the world are home not to the creatures of the mist, but to zoological realities, and 'monster' hunts have taken place everywhere from Sweden to Russia, China and North America. Even a little-known Scottish loch called Loch Ness has got in on the action …

In Cumbria, three lakes have received this attention; Bassenthwaite, Coniston and Windermere. In 1973, a Mr Stavenglass saw a strange, fast-moving animal in Bassenthwaite Lake and took an indistinct, blurred photograph. Whether this was the lake's traditional monster, the Eachy, or a waterfowl or otter, it is difficult to say. As reported in the *Whitehaven News* on 9 July 2008, an angler on the lake landed a pike well over a yard long, and the Keswick Museum has the head of a Bassenthwaite pike that was even larger. In 2007, the team from the Centre for Fortean Zoology ran a brief investigation at Coniston in response to a report that a diver had seen a large eel-like creature, but nothing was found.

It is Windermere, however, that has attracted the monster's share of the attention. The lake, the largest and longest in Cumbria, is 10½ miles long, one mile wide and with a maximum depth of 220ft. A series of well-publicised sightings from 2006 through to 2011 has produced several witness testimonies, a number of intriguing but unconvincing photographs, and a great deal of controversy – many people who have added their comments to on-line news stories, for

The long lake: Lake Windermere looking south from above the town of Windermere.

example, being convinced that some local commercial interests are keeping the monster story in the news just for marketing and tourist revenue purposes.

The flurry of media attention brought forth a hitherto-unknown teratological sighting from the mid-1970s. On 11 September 2010, the *Westmorland Gazette* – the paper that seemed to be making the main running in covering the alleged creature – had an interview with fifty-two-year-old Andrew Bury of Clitheroe, Lancashire. Mr Bury had came forward to describe his experience while fishing on Windermere more than three decades earlier. 'One summer Sunday whilst fishing I was rowing back from Lakeside when I saw a wave along the lake very near to our boat,' he said. 'It was a clear, calm day and it looked as though a boat was dragging along the water, but there was nothing else around that could have caused it. There were seagulls diving all over it and it was moving quite fast. We thought it was really strange. I've spent a lot of time sailing and I've never seen anything like that before.' Note that nothing broke the surface – all he saw was a mysterious wave. And Michael Brook remembered that in the early 1980s he had been standing on the south-western shore of the lake, near Stewardson Nab, when he saw something moving in a straight line close to the opposite shore. He was too far away to see it clearly but by comparing it to a buoy he estimated the object was some three feet high.

The contemporary 'flap' can be conveniently described by a chronological series of incidents:

Incident 1 – 2006. On the hot afternoon of 23 July, Steve and Eileen Burnip were standing on Watbarrow Point, below Wray Castle on the north-western shore of the lake when they saw something moving fast through the water, with three humps – or a head and two humps – breaking the surface. Mr Burnip, on holiday from Hebden Bridge, estimated the total length of

Lake Windermere from the north.

the grey-coloured object as between fifteen and twenty feet, and thought it resembled an eel. Widely reported, this incident set the stamp for subsequent reports.

Incident 2 – 2006. Also in July, Mr and Mrs Gaskell, who regularly boated on the lake, were in their yacht at the entrance to the Ambleside basin, at the north end of Windermere, when they both saw something like a seal or 'a dolphin without the fin.' It surfaced briefly and then dived again without any further reappearance.

Incident 3 – 2007. On 5 February, professional photographer Linden Adams walked up to the summit of Gummers Howe at the southeast corner of the lake with the intention of taking photos of RAF aircraft doing low-level flights at mountain-top height. It was a clear, fine day and the hill offers the best overall view of Lake Windermere. As he waited for the planes to arrive, he and his wife scanned the lake and were astonished to see something large surfacing, diving and resurfacing again off the caravan site of the Hill of Oaks, on the west shore. Despite being well over a mile away, Linden Adams took a number of photographs with his hand-held 300mm lens. He submitted the Raw-format images to Canon, who verified that they had been taken at the time indicated. Mark Carr, an independent forensic photographer, then spent three days analysing the camera's memory card. His conclusion was that the images had not been digitally modified and had not resulted from camera or lens error. Based on the known lengths of objects and locations in the photographs, Carr estimated that the overall shape was around 15m (forty-nine feet) long. When he released the images to the press on 17 February, Linden Adams described the supposed creature as 'Bownessie', after the town of Bowness-on-Windermere. It was a stroke of marketing genius, and virtually every newspaper and television programme since has used the term. Older names for the creature, such as 'Windy' or the 'Bowness Monster', have been elbowed out by media-friendly 'Bownessie'.

Incident 4 – 2007. At the end of February canoeist Michael Bentley claimed to have spotted Bownessie in the southern part of the lake. His report appeared in the *Westmorland Gazette* on 2 March.

Incident 5 – 2007. John Harker wrote to *Practical Photography* magazine (April 2007) about a sighting he had from Langdale Lodge between Windermere and Ambleside. The long underwater shape seemed to showing two small humps just above the surface.

Incident 6 – 2007. On 18 July the *Westmorland Gazette* reported that the crew of a six-tonne yacht moored at the north end of the lake had been awoken by 'a loud banging noise which sent shudders through the vessel'.

Incident 7 – 2008? On 17 March 2011 the *Westmorland Gazette* had a quote from an anonymous elderly fisherman: 'About three years ago I was sailing on my boat when a huge, black, slippery creature came up next to me and rolled over like a huge slab of meat. In twenty years on the lake I'd never seen anything like that before. It gave me the creeps.'

Incident 8 – 2009. Hotelier Thomas Noblett, training in the lake as part of his preparation for a cross-Channel swim, was swamped by a three-foot wave of unknown origin. The incident occurred between 6.45 and 7 a.m., when the lake was empty of people and vessels. The boat being paddled by his swimming trainer was rocked by the wave. 'It was like a big bow wave; a three-foot swell at least,' Mr Noblett told the *Westmorland Gazette* on 23 July. 'There was two, as if a speed boat had sped past, but there were no boats on the lake.'

Incident 9 – 2009. Cameraman John McKeown filmed some 'strange ripples' from the shore while making a documentary about Bownessie in September. They were, it has to be said, somewhat underwhelming.

Incident 10 – unknown date. In September 2009, Karen Walker sent an account of a sighting to John McKeown at Lakes TV. A few years previously she and three others had been on the lake sheltering from a downpour in the small cabin of their boat, when, 'From out of nowhere this dark shadow just under the surface glided past the boat, it never broke the surface of the water; me and my sister-in-law both saw it.'

Incident 11 – 2011. On 16 February Tom Pickles and Sarah Harrington, kayaking on the lake near Belle Isle as part of a corporate team-building training course, saw something 'the size of three cars'. 'At first I thought it was a dog and then saw it was much bigger and moving really quickly at about 10mph,' said Mr Pickles. 'Each hump was moving in a rippling motion and it was swimming fast. I could tell it was much bigger underneath from the huge shadow around it. Its skin was like a seal's but its shape was completely abnormal, not like any animal I've ever seen before.' Ms Harrington compared it to an enormous snake. Mr Pickles took a photograph with his mobile phone. The image, published in the *Westmorland Gazette* on 17 February, had the compulsory 'humps' popularly associated with lake monsters, but to many eyes resembled some kind of inflatable object, like a set of tyres, and staff at the paper have expressed their

Bowness from Belle Isle, approximately the location where the alleged 'Bownessie' image was taken in February 2011.

belief to me that the image is a hoax. On 8 March, the *Gazette* reported the experience of tourist John Phillips, who found some cut-open tyres on a footpath –and when he threw them into the lake, the floating shape looked exactly like Pickle's photograph.

Incident 12 – 2011. On 24 February the *Westmorland Gazette* reported the experience of holidaymakers Brian and June Arton, who saw something 'humped' bobbing up and down in the water off the Beech Hill Hotel on the afternoon of 16 February – the same day as the Belle Isle sighting. Although they were unconcerned about the object, which they took to be a buoy or pontoon, on reading the local paper later they realised that they too may have seen whatever the kayakers had glimpsed.

Reviewing the above it is clear that, for a body of water that is the most visited lake in England, with millions of visitors passing through every year, and daily use by ferries, scheduled cruises, boat charters, yachts and canoeists, the tally of results is utterly, utterly meagre. If there is something large and unknown lurking in Lake Windermere, then those who regularly use the lake would, you suspect, have come up with rather more sightings. You will also notice that several of the incidents are nothing more than descriptions of waves. Large bodies of water like Lake Windermere can behave in ways that seem counter-intuitive. When the water is calm and there is little traffic, the wake from a boat can rebound against the sides and move back into the main body of the water, creating waves that seem to come from nowhere because the boat itself has long moved on. Further, underwater waves known as *seiches* can build up, even if there is no wind, and these too can be experienced without warning. Something that knocks against a boat at night can be a log or piece of jetsam caught up in a *seiche*. In short, natural hydrography

A sturgeon, one of the suggested candidates for the 'Windermere monster'. (From *The Imperial Dictionary*, 1855)

can produce unusual events which can then be *interpreted* as a monster. And in terms of actual sightings, it can be surprising for many people to discover that, under certain viewing conditions, otters, waterbirds, swans and tree-trunks can easily be mistaken for something more mysterious. All these lessons, by the way, have long since been leant by those who study Loch Ness seriously.

But we still have a rump of sightings that cannot be so easily dismissed. Clearly, some people have seen an unusual flesh-and-blood creature. And then there are Linden Adams' photographs. So if there is something beneath the surface, what could it be? Several reports mentioned the possibility of catfish, but these are unlikely to grow large in the cool waters of the Lake District. Pike are known in the area, but they do not grow remotely large enough to fit what has been photographed. The two best possible candidates are an eel or a sturgeon. The latter is a toothless bottom-feeding fish that rarely surfaces, and which, under the right conditions, can live for 100 years at the bottom of European lakes. Its bony backplates (which could easily be mistaken for humps) and grotesque appearance give it a prehistoric quality. If someone introduced a juvenile specimen to the lake several decades ago, it would now be large (and ugly) enough to astonish any witnesses. As for eels, a small proportion of some populations do not migrate back to the Sargasso Sea to spawn and so remain lake-bound. Under these circumstances the sterile creatures, unhampered by the demands of reproducing, grow much larger than usual. The maximum found to date was some fifteen feet long. Perhaps Windermere is home to an exceptionally large specimen. But until someone comes up with a really good quality image that can allow zoological verification, Bownessie remains in the category marked 'Uncertain'.

SEA MONSTERS

In September 2004, Joan Singleton found a bizarre animal corpse on the beach at Parton. It was around four feet long, with the tail of a whale, the body of a seal, claw-like flippers, and sharp

The so-called 'Parton Sea Monster' (actually a desiccated porpoise). (Courtesy of the *Whitehaven News*)

teeth within a beak-like mouth. A photograph of the 'Parton Sea Monster', as it was dubbed, appeared in the *Whitehaven News* on 9 September, and suddenly the internet was awash with monster fever. So many people tried to access the paper's website that its servers crashed. The usual riot of theories, semi-sensible and outlandish, was aired – it was a penguin flayed of its feathers by the waves; it was a decomposed seal pup; it was a radioactive mutant created by a leak from Sellafield; it was a prehistoric sea creature washed up from the depths; and, of course, some claimed that it was an alien.

Fortunately calmer heads prevailed, and marine zoologists from the Natural History Museum in London, Newcastle University and the Centre for Fortean Zoology all independently identified the carcass as a bloated and partially decomposed juvenile harbour porpoise, *Phocoena phocoena*. Decay had stretched the skin around the head, creating a kind of neck, while also shrivelling the flippers into 'claws' and contorting the mouth into a grim and toothy grin. The story continued in the *Whitehaven News* on 16 and 23 September and the *News & Star* on the 15 September, but by now the excitement had largely calmed down. However, when doing a recent internet check I did find one site that claimed the putrescent porpoise was actually a dead baby dragon. Ho hum.

SNAKES

Sometime in 1777 or 1778, a large snake crept into a house at Seaton, near Workington, where it took up residence in a hole in the wall. We are not told just how big this snake was, or where it came from, but it resisted eviction by smoking out with sulphur, and so a former soldier was called in. After waiting patiently for some time he got a chance to strike, and, having trapped the reptile, cut it into pieces which were buried in a hole. The corpse was promptly dug up again by the local people, who believed that the different parts would unite and form a brand new creature. Only when each individual body part was deposited in a separate hole did the neighbourhood breathe easy again. I found the episode in the booklet *The Past People of Allerdale*, which took it from the original in the *Cumberland Chronicle*.

WOLVES AND WEREWOLVES

Putting aside legendary and nonsensical accounts of the 'Last Wolf in England' having been killed at Humphrey Head in South Cumbria, we find at least one authenticated account of a wolf in

Cumbria in modern times. On 10 December 1904, the *Hexham Courant* announced that a wolf was at large in the area around the Northumberland village of Allandale. Over the next few weeks the predator killed around forty sheep, and despite being sighted many times it escaped teams of hunters armed with guns, a pack of foxhounds, and even a 'skilled Indian Game Hunter' named Billy Briddick whose tracking experience in the colonies proved no use. The Hexham Wolf Committee offered a reward for the wolf's corpse, and organised protective measures such as fires lit at night and housing for sheep. For the whole of December Northumberland was in full wolf-panic mode.

Then, on 7 January 1905, the *Courant* stated that on 29 December a wolf had been killed on a railway line at Cumwhinton, a few miles from Carlisle and 30 miles west of Allandale. Photographs and measurements were taking, showing it to be an adult grey wolf four feet eight inches in length with a tail of a further fifteen inches, one foot six inches high at the shoulder, and weighing 5½ stones (35kg). It seemed as if the Hexham Wolf Terror was over. But there was still a mystery to be solved. Ever since the wolf had been first sighted, it was suspected that it was the one that had escaped from the private collection of Captain Bain of Shotley Bridge near Consett. Bain had reported the escape to the police at the time, and, according to *Hexham Herald* of 15 October 1904, the young animal was just four and a half months old and described as 'not much of a threat to either man or beast'. If Bain's account was accurate, then the large wolf found at Cumwhinton could not have been his escapee, and indeed when he inspected the corpse he resolutely stated that it was not his animal. Many commentators have suspected that he actually underestimated its age and size when reporting the loss, and his statement that the Cumwhinton wolf was not his was designed to ensure he would not have to pay compensation for the slaughtered livestock. It is just about possible that there were actually two wolves at large, and indeed over the ensuing few weeks there were further sightings of a wolf around Allendale, although no more livestock were attacked and the reports may have been part if the ongoing wolf-mania. Strangely, no one in Cumbria had reported any wolf sightings before the corpse was found, and Cumwhinton was a long way from the wolf's happy hunting ground in Northumberland. It is nevertheless likely that the Cumwhinton wolf and the Allandale wolf were the same animal, but this cannot be proved.

As for the wolf's body, it was deemed to belong to the owner of the tracks, the Inspector of Ways and Works of the Midland Railway, and the head was mounted and displayed on the wall of the company boardroom in Derby. The Midland ceased to exist in 1923; I have been unable to establish what happened to the wolf's head.

An altogether more spine-chilling tale was related by veteran ghost-hunter Elliott O'Donnell in his 1912 book *Werwolves*. Before giving it, however, I consider it only fair to point out that O'Donnell frequently spiced his many books with episodes that were invented or exaggerated, and as he rarely gives checkable details it is almost impossible when reading his works to distinguish between fact and fiction.

The story concerned a family by the name of Anderson, who, flush with inherited wealth, bought a property somewhere in a remote part of rural Cumberland at the foot of a range of hills. The first hint of trouble was when all their servants quit because they had heard strange noises at night. Then the family's three children reported hearing the sound of wild animals. 'They come howling round the window at night and we hear their feet patter along the passage and stop at our door,' said the oldest son. That night the parents sat up and between two and three o'clock in the morning they too heard what sounded like the growling of a wolf outside the window.

The Allendale wolf. The text on the back of this postcard reads: 'The animal was found cut in two, but was skilfully joined together for the purpose of our photo.' (Author's collection)

Mr. Anderson looked outside but despite it being a pin-sharp moonlit winter's night, could see nothing. When he closed the window the growling recommenced, and worse:

> They heard the front door, which they had locked before coming upstairs, open, and the footsteps of some big, soft-footed animal ascend the stairs. Mr Anderson waited till the steps were just outside the room and then flung open the door, but the light from his acetylene lamp revealed a passage full of moonbeams—nothing else.

Then came Christmas Eve. Mr Anderson dressed up as Santa Claus and just before midnight set out to deliver a sackload of presents. As he approached the children's bedroom he heard the sound of yelping, a sound that grew nearer and extended into snarling and whining. Then when he opened the door, the excited children were appalled to see not just jolly Santa, but also a huge, tall, naked grey figure, 'something like a man with the head of a wolf – a wolf with white pointed teeth and horrid, light eyes.' All were frozen in a tableau of silence and shock until Mrs Anderson appeared with a candle and the ghastly figure vanished. After a sleepless night, the Andersons resolved to sell the house, and moved out as quickly as possible.

So far, so creepy, but then we get into one of O'Donnell's more credulity-stretching paragraphs. He was of the opinion that apparitions such as those experienced by the Andersons were not werewolves as such, but the *ghosts* of werewolves. And this appeared to be backed up by Mr Anderson apparently finding a cave in the hills immediately behind the house. Exploring, he discovered a collection of bones, 'Amongst them was the skull of a wolf, and lying close beside it a human skeleton, with only the skull missing.'

Mr Anderson made the obvious connection – that these were the remains of a werewolf, and that, because the bones had somehow been disturbed, its spirit was now restless. He burnt the bones in the hope of laying the were-ghost to rest.

BLACK DOGS

These supernatural creatures are classic British cryptids (a cryptid being an unknown creature, or an entity that has the shape of an animal). There are dozens of Black Dogs in the folklore of these islands. On occasion they are regarded as death-omens but usually these large, black and uncanny hounds have no precise significance. In Cumbria there are dusty pieces of folklore that identify black dogs as haunting the following locations: Eggholme, on the road between Burneside and Kendal; Endmoor and the Lyth valley, respectively south and west of Kendal; Stainmore, near Kirkby Stephen; on Kell Bank Lane, south of Kirkby Lonsdale; Cappleside Hall and Bela-side Hill, between Beetham and Milnthorpe; Thorny Beck, between St Bees and Sandwith; and around Branthwaite, in Caldbeck.

In 1904, the Revd J. Whiteside recorded in *Shappe in Bygone Days* that the apparition of a black dog was often seen at Shap. In the autumn of 1937, what may have been the same entity was spotted over several nights, running in front of cars at one particular spot on the A6 over Shap Fell, before leaping over a stone parapet into 300ft of empty space above the hillside.

BIG CATS

On the afternoon of 13 October 2009, three staff members in two separate locations saw a large panther-like animal casually stroll across some waste ground adjacent to the Cumberland Infirmary in Carlisle. 'It was absolutely amazing – a lot bigger than a domestic cat and pure black,' dental nurse Sarah Twentyman told the *News & Star* on 17 October. Fellow dental nurse Bonita Curr agreed that it was something out of the ordinary, 'I could see straight away that it was not a domestic cat: it was far too big. The back of its spine was the height of an Alsatian and the head looked like a lynx. It had the elongated body, but it was easily as long as an Alsatian. It just strolled out on to the grass and stood there for a few moments then just ambled away from us.' In total, the sighting lasted about five minutes.

This was an unusual incident – but not because a big cat was spotted. For two decades big cats have been reported from throughout Cumbria. No, what made this episode particularly interesting was that it took place in an urban area in the county's biggest city. By and large most previous big cat reports were from rural or semi-rural areas, so the Cumberland Infirmary sighting may have indicated a change in the behaviour of the Cumbrian big cats.

If, that is, they exist. Official sources and some naturalists routinely deny the possibility that exotic felines are at large in Cumbria. Others are convinced that the beasts are here, and that they are breeding. And some voices claim that these are not creatures of nature, but supernature – that is, they are supernatural.

Analysing the hundreds of reports submitted to the press and big cat websites over the years, it is clear that what witnesses are reporting fall into three distinct categories. There are the large black cats, which bear the closest resemblance to black panthers – these are

The black panther (melanistic leopard). (Leo za1/Wikipedia, licensed under the Creative Commons Attribution–Share Alike 3.0 Unported license)

The North American puma or cougar. (Flickr/Malcolm, licensed under the Creative Commons Attribution–Share Alike 2.0 Generic license)

The Eurasian lynx, with its distinctive tufted ears. (David Castor)

leopards from Asia and Africa with a genetic variant known as melanism, which gives them black coats instead of the usual leopard's spots. Almost as many sightings are of large tan- or sand-coloured animals, which seem to be North American pumas (also known as cougars or mountain lions). A minority of reports describe slightly smaller tawny animals with no obvious tail but tufted ears. These appear to be the Eurasian lynx, which were native to Cumbria up until their extermination around the seventh century AD. These days most lynx are found in Eastern Europe.

Three hypotheses arise as to the identity of these felids (the term for cryptids of a feline nature). The first is that all the sightings – which often are mere glimpses of something odd – are cases of mistaken identity, confusion, and perhaps wish-fulfilment. Certainly this is the case at times. When police searched Wetheral Cemetery after reports of a large cat there in February 2003, they found markings belonging to a fox. In December 2002 it was suggested that several sightings in Furness were down to the misidentification of an unusually well-fed feral domestic cat. Some domestic cat breeds can attain considerable sizes, while under poor lighting conditions it is possible to mistake large dogs for big cats.

A second notion is that the big cats do not leave evidence of their passage because they are in fact paranormal beings that flit out of their Otherworld into ours, to spread confusion and wonder before slipping away into the trans-dimensional nether realms. This was a popular contention in the 1970s and '80s, as it sought to explain why press reports of big cats were often labelled 'FPS' for 'Fruitless Police Search' – obviously such searches would not be able to locate magical beings.

However, we now know a great deal more about big cat behaviour, and the sheer patience and invisibility that can be displayed by leopards in the wild. And, on the side of the 'flesh-and-blood animals' argument, a live puma was trapped in Inverness-shire in 1980, the bodies of several exotic cats have turned up in different parts of the country over the years, and, on a local level, in October 2000 dentist Deborah Davis made plaster casts of two paw prints she found in her garden near Endmoor. Terry Hooper, of the Exotic Animal Register in Bristol, measured the larger print at 8.5 x 10cm – far bigger than the print of a domestic cat – and declared that it was evidence that a big cat had wandered across the fresh soil of Ms Davis' flowerbeds. Plus, of course, there are the hundreds of witness reports, where in a number of cases the sightings lasted for several minutes, allowing for detailed study of the form and behaviour of the animals. Time and again witnesses described the creature as the size of a Labrador or Alsatian, but were adamant that it was neither a dog nor a domestic cat.

As to how the cats got here, most were probably released into the wild in the years following 1976, when the newly-introduced Dangerous Wild Animals Act forced the owners of exotic creatures to not only pay for a licence, but also prove that their pets were secure and well cared for. However big cats can only survive in the wild for a maximum of twenty years, so any animals seen in the past decade – and a great many have been seen – must either be new releases (which are of course illegal), or the creatures are breeding. Indeed, we have evidence that this might be the case. In 1995, two police officers parked up for a mug of coffee at Grizedale Forest saw a pair of what appeared to be black panther cubs.

Of all the strange and exotic things in this book, I suspect that the existence of big cats in Cumbria will be the first element to be actually proved true.

AND FINALLY... RADIOACTIVE GIANT SPIDERS

Back in the 1970s, the presence in Cumbria of the country's largest nuclear reprocessing plant gave rise to a number of jokey 'mutant'-type stories. For example, on 30 June 1978 the Daily Express featured forestry worker Michael King's encounter with a nest of brightly-coloured giant spiders whose webs were steel-like in their tensile strength. The same newspaper (29 January 1979) described how Joe Carr was growing a crop of luminous Pentland Firth potatoes. Needless to say, no one else has found evidence for either of these irradiated freaks of nature.

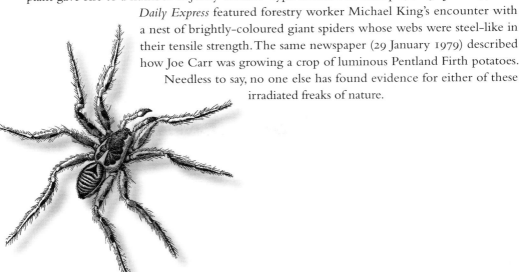

CHAPTER SEVEN

FROM SCARESHIPS TO THE SOLWAY SPACEMAN

SCARESHIPS

In recent years Cumbria has been a veritable powerhouse of UFO sightings, mostly not of 'structured craft' but of 'lights in the sky' – and most 'lights in the sky' are coloured orange or red, which makes them the increasingly popular fire lanterns, and not visitors from Zeta Reticuli. Nevertheless there is still a high degree of unwarranted 'alien fever' in the numerous reports published by the local press. But pause a moment to consider evidence from a previous era, and what it might teach us.

The first airship flew in 1852. Over the next few decades, mystery airships were reported speeding across the skies from various parts of the globe, including the Great Plains of America, the *pampas* of Argentina, and the wilds of New Zealand. The only problem with these reports was that (a) airship technology was primitive and slow, certainly unable to reach the speeds being described, and (b) *there were no actual airships in the areas where they were being reported.* Partly assisted by the fabulous fantasies of Jules Verne (such as *Robur the Conqueror, or The Clipper of the Clouds*, 1886, and *Master of the World*, 1904), airships had captured the public imagination, and imagination then populated the skies with non-existent airships. Later researchers have dubbed these imaginary craft 'scareships'. By the time Count von Zeppelin flight-tested his first 'air battleship' in 1900, the airship was a fixture in the mass mindscape, a 'bogey' figure that held *fin-de-siècle* society in a similar grip to the way nuclear weapons dominated the apocalyptic dreams of the late twentieth century.

So in hindsight it was perhaps no surprise that when a state of war was announced between Britain and Germany on 4 August 1914, and a holocaust of Zeppelin-led bombing was expected daily, the British public started reporting sightings of German airships and winged aircraft almost immediately. But, once again, there was a disjunction with reality: German aerial technology was more limited than was generally believed, and the first air-raid did not take place until Christmas Day 1914 (on Kent) while the first Zeppelin attack (on Norfolk) occurred on the night of 19/20 January 1915. For the early years of the war, the vast majority of the British Isles was beyond the range of the German airships and bombers.

The first flight of a Zeppelin, on Lake Geneva. (From *Pearson's Magazine,* Vol. X, July-Dec 1900)

So during the early months of the war there were no Zeppelins, and there were no German raiders. But that did not prevent a great many people from seeing them, as recorded in a file in the National Archives (AIR 1/565 16/15/89), entitled *GHQ Home Forces General Correspondents File: Movements and Rumoured Movements of Hostile Aircraft Etc., 3/8/14-2/1/15.* (For this section, I am deeply indebted to Nigel Watson's superbly researched 2000 book *The Scareship Mystery*, especially the chapter 'Dangerous Rumours: First World War Scares in Britain' by Granville Oldroyd.) One of the first reports came from Cumbria, on 5 August 1914, just one day after war was declared. At 2.45 a.m., a pair of water bailiffs on the River Eden reported the sound of an unseen aircraft apparently following the course of the river. So far so ominous – but then reports started to pile up around Barrow-in-Furness, home to the Vickers shipbuilding yard and thus of incalculable importance to the war effort. On the night of 7 August, the air-raid sirens wailed above Barrow and all the lights at the factory were switched off as a precaution. On the night of 9 August, at the Next Ness Bridge by Ulverston, two privates of the King's Own (Royal Lancaster) Regiment, and two civilians of good standing, all heard a buzzing sound high in the air, accompanied by a bright light – and one of the witnesses saw the unmistakable shape of an airship once the light went out, heading towards Barrow. Around the same time an airship was reported following a train from Askam to Bootle, while on the night of 10/11 August both the Army commander of Barrow Defences and the Royal Navy commander of the airship shed at Barrow reported sightings of at least two Zeppelins. This was all during the first week of the war – and of course there were no hostile aircraft in Cumbrian skies.

The war fever continued to power a host of erroneous sightings. On 11 and 12 August, a police sergeant and two constables heard an aircraft flying above Egremont and saw strange moving lights over the Solway Firth. A sentry at Barrow reported another light in the sky while the Chief Constable, no less, saw an unexplained stationary light over Carlisle. An airship was spotted over Penrith on 14 August, and aircraft were reported from Eskdale, Brandling Ghyll near Cockermouth, Parton by Whitehaven, Uldale, and Carlisle.

By now a full-scale panic was afflicting many people in Cumbria, with hundreds of binoculars and telescopes trained on the skies, and sightings flooding in. Hills and glens were being searched for secret fuel dumps. Foreigners were being stopped and interrogated. On 17

August, Barrow – which had the only anti-aircraft gun on the northwest coast – was authorised to fire on any approaching airship. The following day, aircraft were reported from Great Orton, Aspatria, Crosby-on-Eden, Houghton, Loweswater and Ireby near Wigton. On the night of 19/20 August, a soldier saw an aeroplane flying near the ground between Flimby and Siddick, heading along the coast near Workington. The following two nights a craft was heard flying above Seaton, near Workington, in the direction of St Bees Head. Further sightings came in from Seascale, and Lynhow near Carlisle, which were by and large the end of the Cumbrian 'flap'. Sightings of enemy aircraft then sprang up in Galloway, Perthshire, Liverpool and many other locations. No enemy aircraft was ever found, and almost a century of archival digging has failed to uncover any trace of the alleged secret fuel-dumps, airfields and planning involved in any covert aerial operation. Stated bluntly, not a single one of the hundreds of airships and aeroplanes reported over Britain in the first five months of the war were real.

Several interesting details can be gleaned from the mass of reports in Cumbria. Firstly, sightings were being communicated from all classes, with solicitors, estate owners and society ladies competing with chauffeurs, soldiers and miners. So social standing or professional status were no guarantee of accurate reporting – something to bear in mind when we are told to always believe contemporary UFO witnesses, 'because why would they lie?' Secondly, only a minority of witnesses actually claimed to have seen a physical aircraft – most simply reported unusual lights, something which again has resonance with modern sightings, which are mostly of strange lights. Thirdly, the number of sightings peaked just after a report of one appeared in the local newspapers. And, even during the credulous first weeks of the war, some sightings – including one by a minor aristocrat – were investigated and found to be misperceptions of natural night-time denizens such as the planet Jupiter or bright stars – yet another parallel with later UFO sightings, a surprising number of which turn out to be Sirius, Venus, or even the Moon.

Finally – once again like today – we further discover that sceptical commentators thought that the flap was due to psycho-social factors, and nothing to do with actual nuts-and-bolts aircraft. On 3 September, a Major de Wattevill drafted a communication to the War Office from the headquarters of Mersey Defences (Liverpool):

> The airship scares continue harmlessly. The Chief Constable of Lancashire is clean off his head over them. He has enlisted 20,000 special PCs for the war and they have to earn their living. I am convinced that Barrow is cracked on the subject. There are so many iron foundries in Furness that at night the glare of the smoke in the sky are enough to create airships whenever the winds & clouds are right.

And in March 1916 the War Office issued a circular denouncing the role of unfounded rumours in wartime:

> Observers reporting the presence of hostile aircraft have in repeated instances been unduly influenced, if not led into absolute hallucination, by the unnecessary communication to them by higher authority of information pointing to the very doubtful presence of aircraft in their vicinity. Reports and rumours thus repeated acquire precision and become magnified in circulation; they soon assume the form of definite statements that hostile airships have been actually seen in various localities.

As a slightly cheeky exercise, I took this report and removed all references to 'aircraft', replacing them with more contemporary, post-Roswell, phraseology:

> Observers reporting the presence of *UFOs* have in repeated instances been unduly influenced, if not led into absolute hallucination, by the unnecessary communication to them by *media sources and true believers* of information pointing to the very doubtful presence of *extraterrestrials* in their vicinity. Reports and rumours thus repeated acquire precision and become magnified in circulation; they soon assume the form of definite statements that *alien spacecraft* have been actually seen in various localities.

Hmmm. I rest my case.

THE SOLWAY SPACEMAN

It is one of the great 'mystery photographs' of all time. It is 24 May 1964. A six-year-old girl sits outside on a sunny day in her new dress, holding a posy of flowers. And behind her, looming ominously in the background, is a strange figure who appears to be wearing a spacesuit. The image of the 'Solway Spaceman' has intrigued and baffled ever since.

The image of his daughter, Elizabeth, was taken by Carlisle fireman Jim Templeton on the estuarine marshlands around Burgh-by-Sands, on the Solway Firth west of Carlisle. At the time

he noticed nothing unusual, and is adamant that no one else was nearby on the flat, open landscape at the time he took the photograph. The figure only came to light when Jim received the pictures from the developers. Jim had the photo tested by his contacts at the police, and then by the film's manufacturers, Kodak. Both declared the image genuine – that is, the negative had not been tampered with – but puzzling, and Kodak later offered free film for life to anyone who could solve the enigma. The subsequent

The famous photograph of the so-called Solway or Cumberland Spaceman, taken on 24 May 1964. (Courtesy of Jim Templeton)

publicity made Jim (and Elizabeth) media celebrities, but the attention affected the little girl's nerves so badly that she had to be withdrawn from school for a time. This, plus the fact that Jim Templeton has never made any money from the hundreds of times the photograph has been reproduced in everything from books to television programmes, tells us that we are not dealing with a straightforward hoax perpetuated by the Templeton family.

So what is the mystery figure? There are as many hypotheses as they are hypothesists, but from the very start it should be noted that the figure has only been dubbed a 'spaceman' (and hence linked with the ever-expanding UFO mythos) because it *appears* to be wearing an astronaut-type space helmet and, by extension, a spacesuit. It should also be pointed out that the figure is very slightly out of focus, a consequence of the depth of field and quality of the 50mm lens on Jim's 35mm SLR camera. Using the known properties of such lenses, it has been calculated that the figure is some twelve or fifteen feet behind Elizabeth.

Assuming that the white-garbed figure is not an extraterrestrial, an inter-dimensional voyager or a time-traveller who has just happened to wander through the background while an amateur photographer was setting up, a number of more reasonable suggestions have been put forward:

1. The white shape is a distorted view of a seagull or other seabird in flight.

2. It is a piece of litter being blown by the wind. There was a breeze at the time, as can be seen by the movement in Elizabeth's hair.

3. It is a fake, a composite image constructed by some kind of superimposition technique. This was the conclusion drawn by Roger Green of Bradford University, who analysed the image for *UFO Magazine* (May-June 1997). In their 2002 book *Out of the Shadows*, UFO investigators David Clarke and Andy Roberts speculate that the superimposition may have been created by someone in the local film processing lab, perhaps as some kind of joke.

4. It is an actual human being. In a persuasive argument on his blog, Gordon Hudson looked closely at the figure. Although on first glance it appears to be someone in a helmet looking towards the viewer, Mr Hudson suggested that the pose, bodyshape and angle of the visible elbow all show a person with their back to the camera. The 'helmet' is actually the back of a hood. The conclusion is that it was a human being wearing a white hooded coat walking away from the camera. As viewfinders on SLR cameras were very restricted at that date, vision was limited and therefore it was possible not to notice someone briefly appearing in the background.

All these suggestions are of course just that — suggestions. Perhaps the real solution will never be known. In the end, all we are left with is that iconic, enigmatic photograph.

We started this book with one enduring Cumbrian mystery, the Croglin Vampire, and finish it with another. Wonders and marvels still surround us, it seems.

BIBLIOGRAPHY

BOOKS

Anon, *Legends of Westmorland and The Lake District* (Hamilton B. Adams; London/Rawson B. Lee; Kendal, 1874)

Alexander, Marc, *Haunted Churches & Abbeys of Britain* (Arthur Baker; London, 1978)

Allerdale Borough Council, *The Past People of Allerdale: Tales and stories of the interesting and famous people of West Cumbria* (Allerdale Borough Council; Workington, n.d.)

Anderson, Robert, *Ballads in the Cumberland Dialect* (W. Davison; Alnwick, n.d. 1840?)

Ashbridge, Ian, *Foul Deeds & Suspicious Deaths In & Around Carlisle* (Wharncliffe Books; Barnsley, 2006)

Ashton, John, *The Devil in Britain and America* (Ward and Downey; London, 1896)

Askew, John, *Guide to Cockermouth* (Isaac Evening; Cockermouth, 1872 – facsimile reprint by The Printing House; Cockermouth, 2000)

Beloff, John, 'A Note on a Putatively Precognitive Disaster Dream' in *Journal of the Society for Psychical Research*, Vol. 49 (1977–1978)

Bord, Janet, *The Traveller's Guide to Fairy Sites* (Gothic Image; Glastonbury, 2004)

Bouch, C.M.L., *Prelates and People of the Lake Counties* (T. Wilson; Kendal, 1948)

Briggs, Katharine M., *A Dictionary of British Folk-Tales in the English Language* (Routledge and Kegan Paul; London, 1971)

Brooks, J.A., *Ghosts and Legends of the Lake District* (Jarrold Publishing; Norwich, 1988)

Bulmer, T. F., *History, Topography & Directory of Cumberland* (T. Bulmer & Co.; Penrith, 1901)

Burn, Peter, *English Border Ballads* (G. & T. Coward; Carlisle/Bemrose & Sons, London, 2nd edition, 1877)

Burns, William E., *An Age of Wonders: Prodigies, politics and providence in England 1657–1727* (Manchester University Press; Manchester, 2002)

Carruthers, F.J., *Lore of the Lake Country* (Robert Hale; London, 1975)

Clarke, David & Roberts, Andy, *Out of the Shadows: UFOs, the Establishment & the Official Cover-Up* (Piatkus; London, 2002)

Cleaver, Alan & Park, Lesley, *On the Hunt of Fairies in Cumbria* (Alan Cleaver; Whitehaven, 2010)

———————— *Witches & Witchcraft* (Alan Cleaver; Whitehaven, 2010)

———————— *Wizards & Wizardry* (Alan Cleaver; Whitehaven, 2010)

Clive-Ross, F., 'The Croglin Vampire' in *Tomorrow* Vol. XI. No. 11 (Spring 1963)

Cooper, Joe, *The Case of the Cottingley Fairies* (Robert Hale; London, 1990)

Cowper, Henry Swainson, *Hawkshead: (The Northernmost Parish of Lancashire) Its History, Archaeology, Industries, Folklore, Dialect, Etc.* (Bemrose & Sons; London and Derby, 1899)

———————— 'Witchcraft, and Traditional Customs' in *Transactions of the Cumberland and Westmorland Antiquarian and Archaeological Society* Vol. 14 (1897)

Devereux, Paul, *Fairy Paths and Spirit Roads* (Vega Books; London, 2003)

Dickinson, William, *Cumbriana or, Fragments of Cumbrian Life* (Whittaker & Co, London/Callander & Dixon; Whitehaven, 1876)

Ewen, C. L'Estrange, *Witchcraft and Demonism* (Heath Cranton; London, 1933)

Fanthorpe, Lionel & Fanthorpe, Patricia *The World's Greatest Unsolved Mysteries* (Hounslow Press; Toronto, 1997)

Ferguson, Richard S., (ed.) *The Royal Charters of the City of Carlisle* (C. Thurnam & Sons; Carlisle/ T. Wilson; Kendal / Elliot Stock; London, 1894)

Ferguson, Richard S., *Diocesan Histories: Carlisle* (SPCK; London, 1889)

Ferrol, Stuart, 'The Hexham Wolf' in *Fortean Times* 192 (January 2005)

Findler, Gerald, *Legends of the Lake Counties* (Dalesman; Clapham, 1967)

————*Ghosts of the Lake Counties* (Dalesman; Kendal, 1969)

Fort, Charles, *The Book of the Damned* (John Brown Publishing; London, New Ed. 1995)

————*Lo!* (John Brown Publishing; London, New Ed. 1997)

Fraser, George MacDonald, *The Steel Bonnets: The Story of the Anglo-Scottish Border Reivers* (Collins Harvill; London, 1971)

Fraser, Mark (ed.), *Big Cats in Britain Yearbook 2006* (CFZ Press; Bideford, 2006)

————*Big Cats in Britain Yearbook 2007* (CFZ Press; Bideford, 2007)

Freeman, Richard, 'The Sea Freak of Parton' in *Animals and Men* No.35 (2004)

Gurney, Edmund, Frederic W. H. Myers & Frank Podmore *Phantasms of the Living* (The Society for Psychical Research/ Trubner & Co., London, 1886)

Hare, Augustus J.C., *The Story of My Life* Volume IV (George Allen; London, 1900)

Harper, Charles G., *Haunted Houses* (Cecil Palmer; London, 1907)

Henderson, William, *Folklore of the Northern Counties of England and the Borders* (The Folk-lore Society/ W. Satchell, Peyton & Co.; London, 1879)

Hodgson, Mrs., 'On some Surviving Fairies' in *Transactions of the Cumberland and Westmorland Antiquarian and Archaeological Society* New Series Vol. 1 (1901)

Hodson, Geoffrey, *Fairies at Work and at Play* (The Theosophical Publishing House; London, 1957 – first published 1925)

————*The Kingdom of Faerie* (The Theosophical Publishing House; London, 1927)

————*Angels And The New Race* (The Theosophical Publishing House; London, 1929)

Holder, Geoff *The Guide to the Mysterious Lake District* (The History Press; Stroud, 2009)

Hulme, Frederick Edward, *Natural History Lore and Legend* (Bernard Quaritch; London, 1895)

Hutchinson, William, *The History of the County of Cumberland* 2 Vols. (F. Jollie; Carlisle, 1794)

Hutton, Ronald, *The Triumph of the Moon* (Oxford University Press; Oxford, 2001)

Menefee, Samuel Pyeatt, 'Circling as an Entrance to the Otherworld' in *Folklore*, Vol. 96, No. 1 (1985)

Myers, Frederic W. H., *Human Personality and Its Survival of Bodily Death* (Longmans, Green, & Co.; London, 1903)

Newman, L.F., and E.M. Wilson, 'Folk-Lore Survivals in the Southern "Lake Counties" and in Essex: A Comparison and Contrast' in *Folklore*, Vol. 62, No. 1 (March 1951), Vol. 63, No. 2 (June 1952) and Vol. 64, No. 1 (March 1953)

Nightingale, B., *The Ejected of 1662 in Cumberland & Westmorland* (Sherratt & Hughes; Manchester & London, 1911)

O'Donnell, Elliott, *Werwolves* (Methuen & Co.; London, 1912)

Oldroyd, Granville, 'Dangerous Rumours: First World War Scares in Britain' in Watson, Nigel (ed.), *The Scareship Mystery: A Survey of Worldwide Phantom Airship Scares (1909-1918)* (Domra Publications; Corby, 2000)

Rabinovitch, Shelley and James Lewis, *The Encyclopedia of Modern Witchcraft and Neo-paganism* (New York Citadel Press; New York, 2002)

Rowling, Marjorie, *The Folklore of the Lake District* (B.T. Batsford; London, 1976)

Scott, Daniel, *Bygone Cumberland and Westmorland* (William Andrews & Co.; London, 1899)

Screeton, Paul, *Quicksilver Heritage* (Thorsons Publishers; Wellingborough; 1974)

Sharpe, James, *Instruments of Darkness: Witchcraft in England 1550-1750* (Hamish Hamilton; London, 1996)

Shuker, Karl, 'British Mystery Cats – The Bodies of Evidence' in *Fortean Studies* Vol. 2 (John Brown Publishing; London, 1995)

Smith, Colin Brookes, 'Some Long-range ESP Propagation Experiments' in *Journal of the Society for Psychical Research* Vol. 48 (1975-1976)

Sullivan, Jeremiah, *Cumberland and Westmorland, Ancient and Modern: The People, Dialect, Superstitions and Customs* (London; Whittaker, 1857)

Summers, Montague, *The Vampire in Europe* (E.P. Dutton & Co.; New York, 1929)

Underwood, Peter, *The Vampire's Bedside Companion* (Leslie Frewin Publishers; London, 1974)

White, John Pagen, *Lays and Legends of the English Lake Country* (G. and T. Coward; Carlisle, and John Russell Smith; London, 1873)

Wilson, Thomas, *The Pitman's Pay, and Other Poems* (William Douglas; Gateshead/Charnley; Newcastle / Simpkin, Marshall & Co.; London, 1843)

Whiteside, Joseph, *Shappe in Bygone Days* (Titus Wilson; Kendal, 1904)

Whittington-Egan, Richard, 'The Croglin Vampire' in *Contemporary Review* (June 2005)

Wood, J.G., *Bible Animals; Being a Description of Every Living Creature Mentioned in the Scriptures, from the Ape to the Coral* (Longmans, Green & Co.; London, 1883)

JOURNALS

Journal of the Society for Psychical Research:Vol. 6 (1893-1894);Vol. 10 (1901-1902);Vol. 19 (1919-1920)

Monthly Magazine and British Register: Vol.15 (1803)

Proceedings of the Society for Psychical Research:Vol. 10 (1894)

NEWSPAPERS AND MAGAZINES *(*indicates Big Cat report)*

Cumberland News: 25 February 2005; 1, 4, 11, 13 & 18 March 2005; 22 February 2010; 3 August 2010*; 10 August 2010; 24 September 2010; 10 December 2010

Daily Express: 30 June 1978; 29 January 1979

Daily Mail: 3 & 8 March 2005

Daily Telegraph: 21 May 1965; 4 November 2001

Fortean Times No. 277, July 2011

Guardian: 9 March 2005

Hexham Courant: 10 December 1904; 7 January 1905

Hexham Herald: 15 October 1904

Life: November 1964

News & Star: 15 September 2004; 1, 3-10, 14 & 29 March 2005; 19 January 2006; 22 March 2006*; 12 January 2007; 15 & 21 September 2009; 17 October 2009*

North West Evening Mail: 31 August 2002*; 16 July 2008

Practical Photography:April 2007

Sunday Telegraph 3 May 1964; 6 March 1988*

Sunday Times: 27 October 1963; 6 March 2005

The Times: 3 June 1966; 31 October 1966; 1 November 1966; 6 June 1993*; 2 March 2005; 25 February 2010

Times & Star: 11 March 2005

Tit-Bits: 4 June 1964

Westmorland Gazette: 2000 – 1 January*; 6, 13 & 27 October*; 1 December*; 2001 – 23 February*; 10 August*; 23 & 29 November*; 2002 – 25 January*; 16 & 19 April*; 5 July*; 16 August*; 5, 8 & 15 November*; 8, 20 & 27 December*; 2003 – 3, 14, 17 & 20 January*; 13 & 28 March*; 3 April*; 1 August*; 24 October*; 2004 – 13 March*; 28 April*; 7 May*; 23 July*; 8 October*; 2005 – 4 & 9 March*; 22 April*; 3 June*; 2 & 23 September*; 2006 – 31 January*; 29 March*; 28 July*; 4 & 11 August*; *2007* - 2 February*; 2 March; 18 July; 5 December*; 2008 – 5, 22 & 27 September*; 2009 – 23 July; 28 August*; 2 September*; 2010 – 11 September; 2011 – 3 February*; 17 & 24 February; 8 & 17 March

Whitehaven News: 9, 16 & 23 September 2004; 22 May 2008; 9 July 2008; 13 October 2010; 19 January 2011

WEBSITES

Big Cats in Britain: www.bigcatsinbritain.org

Centre for Fortean Zoology: www.cfz.org.uk

Gordon Hudson: www.ecalpemos.org/2010/01/cumberland-spaceman.html

Linden Adams: www.lindenadamsphotography.co.uk

INDEX